BOMB CHILDREN

BOMB CHILDREN

Life in the Former Battlefields of Laos

———

LEAH ZANI

Duke University Press · *Durham and London* · 2019

© 2019 Duke University Press
All rights reserved
Printed in the United States of America on acid-free paper ∞
Designed by Courtney Leigh Baker and typeset in Whitman and
Rockwell by Westchester Publishing Services

Library of Congress Cataloging-in-Publication Data
Names: Zani, Leah, [date] author.
Title: Bomb children : life in the former battlefields
of Laos / Leah Zani.
Description: Durham : Duke University Press, 2019. |
Includes bibliographical references and index.
Identifiers: LCCN 2018052743 (print)
LCCN 2019010347 (ebook)
ISBN 9781478005261 (ebook)
ISBN 9781478004226 (hardcover : alk. paper)
ISBN 9781478004851 (pbk. : alk. paper)
Subjects: LCSH: Vietnam War, 1961–1975—Campaigns—Laos. |
Vietnam War, 1961–1975—Aerial operations, American. |
Laos—History—1975– | Unexploded ordnance—
Social aspects—Laos. | Cluster bombs—Laos. |
Land mine victims—Laos. | Ethnology—Laos. |
Laos—Rural conditions—Poetry.
Classification: LCC DS557.8.L3 (ebook)
LCC DS557.8.L3 Z36 2019 (print) |
DDC 959.704/31—dc23
LC record available at https://lccn.loc.gov/2018052743

COVER ART: Cluster munitions, COPE Centre, Vientiane, Laos.
© Godong/Alamy Stock Photo.

Contents

Acknowledgments

I thank Courtney Berger, my editor at Duke University Press, for her editorial guidance, faith in my authorship, and support of this book. I am indebted to the editorial staff, marketing staff, and anonymous reviewers at Duke whose feedback greatly improved this book.

My deepest thanks to Tom Boellstorff, Jennifer Terry, and Mei Zhan for reading and commenting on early versions of this book. I am grateful to the members of my writing group for their expert reading and thinking: Alyse Bertenthal, Jessica Cooper, Cheryl Deutsch, Lizzy Hare, Georgia Hartman, Natalie Valdez, and Anna Zogas. The research and writing of this book occurred through various intellectual communities, including the Working Collective on Geographies of Care and Intervention at the University of California (Irvine); the Center for Ethnography at Irvine; and the Access Asia group at Irvine. I extend thanks to the poets of the Society for Humanistic Anthropology, with special care for Melisa Cahnmann-Taylor, Nomi Stone, and Ather Zia. I am grateful to the members of these intellectual and creative communities for our many discussions, presentations, poetry readings, and informal peer reviews.

Thanks to the many, and wonderful, people whom I delighted in thinking with over the course of this project: Chima Anyadike-Danes, Michael Boddington, Colin Cahill, Nigel Chang, Darcie DeAngelo, Jo Durham, Julia Elyachar, Nick Enfield, Grant Evans, Padma Govindan, Robin Hamilton-Coates, Holly High, Andreas Hofmann, Angela Jenks, Eleana Kim, George Marcus, Warren Mayes, Kimberley McKinson, Megan Neal, Valerie Olson, Shannon Parris, Kristin Peterson, Beth Reddy, Jason Rolan, Eli Simon, Sarinda Singh, Kathryn Sweet, Eric Stover, Vinya Sysamouth, Mindy Tauberg, Heather Thomas, Krisna Uk, Jeff Wasserstrom, Rebecca Wilbanks, and Sheron Wray. I extend special thanks to my research hosts in Laos, who remain anonymous; and to my wonderful Lao research assistant, who remains anonymous. In line with my confidentiality agreements and subject protections, many remain unnamed—which sharpens my gratitude and admiration.

I am grateful for the care and love of my partners, friends, and family over the course of this project—with special thanks to my husband, Alexandre Zani, for his emotional and financial support.

An abbreviated version of chapter 1 appeared in *Anthropology and Humanism* (2018), and I previously discussed my concept of bomb ecologies in *Somatosphere* (2015) and *Environmental Humanities* (2018). I have presented earlier versions of this work at a number of conferences, including the 2017 Militarized Ecologies Workshop with the Sawyer Center Documenting War at the University of California (Irvine); the 2017 Geography Colloquium at the University of California (Berkeley); the 2015 Southeast Asian Studies Symposium at Sunway University; and the 2015 EuroSEAS conference at the University of Vienna; as well as the American Anthropological Association annual meetings in San Jose 2018, Washington, DC, 2017, Minneapolis 2016, and Denver 2015. I am grateful for the insightful comments and conversation of the scholars at these events, all of which contributed to a better book.

The research and writing for this book were funded by the National Science Foundation, the Human Rights Center at the University of California (Berkeley), the Center for Global Peace and Conflict Studies at the University of California (Irvine), the Center for Asian Studies at Irvine, the Department of Anthropology at Irvine, and the Center for Lao Studies. My graduate training was supported by a National Science Foundation Graduate Research Program Fellowship and a Social Sciences Merit Fellowship.

Note on the Lao Language

There are no standard transliterations between Lao and English words. I have used colloquial translations and transliterations when available (for example, the word "karma" instead of *kamma*) to aid the reader in recognizing more familiar terms. Unless a colloquial transliteration in English already exists, I have tried to preserve consonant distinctions and vowel lengths in my transliterations (for example, transliterating "development" as the conventional *phattana* rather than the more accurate *phatthanaa*).

Lao naming practices do not follow the Western norm of personal first name then formal last name. In Lao, it is common to refer to a person more formally by a first name, particularly in honorifics. I have respected this by citing Lao authors by their first names in in-text citations and in the reference list—unless the author has published significantly in English under their last name. All other authors are cited by their last names.

FIELDPOEM 30
Postwar

My sight has changed forever:
I see the hulk of an army-green
helicopter
in a farm field in rural California
amongst rusting tractors, threshers
harvesters

Every one is a wreck of something

Introduction

—

THE FRUIT EATERS

Opening Invocation

Before becoming a bomb technician, an interlocutor of mine served as a monk for seven years at a Theravada Buddhist temple in Vientiane, the capital of Laos. After his workday at the office of an explosives clearance operator that is hosting my research, he invites me to ride with him on his motorbike to visit his former temple, Wat Sokpaluang, on the outskirts of town. Wat Sokpaluang is a forest temple, originally situated in the jungle outside the city walls—though in recent decades it has been fully encompassed by urban sprawl. The temple maintains expansive forested grounds, circumnavigated by a white, gilded wall. Leaving our motorbike beyond the wall, we enter by foot under a large, lavishly painted archway of entwined dragons. As we cross into the forested interior, the sound of the nearby thoroughfare is smothered by the vestigial forest preserved within the temple grounds: an underbrush of flowering ginger and medicinal herbs, plus large trees whose trunks host pale lichens, wax-leaved bromeliads, ferns, and trailing gray lianas. When we arrive at the central plaza next to the *sim* (the most sacred central building), a cremation is under way (see figure I.1). The relatives and guests have left—only two silent novices remain to tend the giant kiln. They kindle the

FIGURE I.1 A cremation under way at Wat Sokpaluang. Photo by the author.

fire with long sticks, producing snapping crackles that seem only to deepen the silence in the plaza. The air is suffused with blue smoke and the thick smell of incense. The coffin has already collapsed upon itself, and the body is no longer visible within the flames. Wreaths and other flower decorations smoke, their green moisture resisting the cremation. We stay at the border of the plaza and watch the flames slowly diminish the corpse and the flowers.

In this quiet zone of mortal reflection, my companion tells me a strange, brief war story he heard while he was a monk at this temple. He told this story in the present tense, as he first heard it and as I tell it here: Two American soldiers are flying a helicopter low over the jungles of Laos, scouting for villages during the Vietnam-American War. They are looking for possible communist hideouts, sites where rebels built camps or were hosted by existing villages. Skimming the treetops, one soldier very clearly sees a village below: grass huts on stilts, dirt-worn paths through the green fields, people walking with baskets of fruit strapped to their backs. He signals a landing nearby, but once they are on the ground, there is no village to be found. After giving up the search and reboarding their helicopter, the two soldiers keep watch out of the vehicle's windows. Neither one sees a village. The village and its inhabitants have disappeared.

In response to my perplexed expression, my interlocutor explains, "There are worlds around us that we can't see, full of people who are right and honest and only eat fruit. They never kill anything." These worlds exist parallel to the present realm: other realms, other heavens and hells. My interlocutor spreads his arms wide and sweeps them around while wriggling his fingers as if to touch the stuff of these many worlds all around us, invisible. The world that the soldiers glimpsed in the war story is known as the realm of the fruit eaters. It is a special paradise inhabited by merit-filled beings who never kill anything to sustain themselves; they only eat fruit that has fallen freely from wild trees. This kind of food is free from the negative karma of slaughtering animals or destroying plants. It is a realm without butchers, meat eaters, murderers, executioners, or soldiers. As a result of the virtuous habits of the residents, the realm of the fruit eaters is peaceful, and all the beings who reside there are healthy and happy. Only especially morally correct beings are reincarnated as fruit eaters. By comparison, the immoral actions of the inhabitants of our world are creating a state of near-perpetual war, violence, and suffering. My interlocutor explains that the Vietnam-American War made the boundaries between these parallel worlds porous; and so, in the midst of war, one American soldier glimpses a Lao paradise free of violence.

I call it a strange war story since it isn't really a war story at all—it is a story about a world of peace, present but out of reach to all but the exceedingly virtuous. The realm of the fruit eaters was closed to the soldiers due to their immoral actions during war, but the war had also, paradoxically, brought such worlds closer to ours. Lao political cosmology exhibits a form of "this-worldly and otherworldly parallelism" in which political systems are "doubled" in our world and in other, parallel worlds (Holt 2009, 44). These other, parallel realms legitimize this-worldly political systems—for example, by ritually confirming the parity between the spirit world and our own. In this logic of parallels, the perception of other realms of peace may be interpreted as evidence of the immorality of our political systems—while also indicating that alternate forms of politics are possible. The fruit eaters' realm of ultimate peace was visible, but not equally visible to everyone. Only one soldier could see it. And my interlocutor, gesturing around us with his arms outstretched, was indicating that the two of us couldn't see it. I invoke this war story now, at the beginning of this book, as an invitation to look past war to other possible worlds—to learn to perceive peace just out of reach.

The Sociality of War

To examine the long-term social and cultural impact of war is to confront the fundamental sociality of war. This requires dismantling binaries between war and peace and instead examining war and its aftermath as constitutive parts of larger, ongoing processes of social change. Processes of "slow violence" and "long dying" (Nixon 2006–7, 14), in which violence prolongs itself via subtle and pervasive effects, may far exceed the historical boundaries of war. At the same time, the effects of war are not limited to violence and destruction: conflict zones are key sites for economic intervention, human rights advocacy, and humanitarian assistance (Fassin 2012; Redfield 2005; Rosenblatt 2015), as well as spaces of alternative or underground social, political, and economic forms (Nordstrom 2004). Following this tradition, I assert that war is not an aberration from the social, but is constitutive of modern forms of political control, economic transformation, and social action. Countering assumptions that war destroys society, in this book I examine the former battlefields of Laos as social fields powerfully shaped by violence and intervention. In the transition from battlefield to marketplace, or minefield to schoolyard, the reconstruction and rehabilitation practices that attend war constitute crucial acts of political and social intervention.

Contemporary Laos is one of the most rapidly developing countries in the world; it is also the world's most bombed country, per capita, and remains massively contaminated with explosive military wastes from the Vietnam-American War. This book examines the present period of rapid development and revival amid these exploding remnants of war. In the 1960s and 1970s, Laos was subject to a massive air war and counterinsurgency program as part of an American paramilitary operation run by the Central Intelligence Agency (CIA) in secret and without the knowledge of Congress. Generally known as the Secret War, the conflict in Laos was the longest and most intense air war in history (i.e., a war fought primarily with air power and minimal ground troops; see Branfman 2013). Cluster munitions, land mines, mortar shells, and other military waste continued to explode after the war ended, and will continue to explode for centuries. These remnants of war embed themselves in people's everyday lives far beyond the cessation of conflict. What are the long-term social and cultural impacts of military waste, particularly in the context of covert warfare? How do people build lives in former battlefields and interact with explosive remnants of war? How is ongoing war violence incorporated into peacetime development?

In response to these concerns, I develop a conceptual framework for parallelism, or the treatment of war's violent remains and postwar revival as parallel, layering, but also often distinct, phenomena. I use the paired concepts of remains and revivals to analyze the sedimentation of war and peace as a feature of contemporary geopolitics. By "remains," I refer to massive military wastes left over from the Secret War. In the explosives clearance sector, explosive remnants of war is a technical term describing ordnance that remains after a conflict has ended. My use of the term "remains" refers not only to these physical remains of war but also to sociocultural phenomena produced by war and its aftermath. By "revivals," I refer to several interweaving processes in postwar Laos: socioeconomic liberalization, authoritarian renovation, and religious awakening. I use the term "revivals" to reference the layering of old and new that characterizes contemporary Lao nation building; for example, the revival of a romanticized prewar Lao state within the Party state's socialist reforms. "Revivals" also references the ongoing transformation of military waste after war, such as the scavenging of bombs for sale in the illegal war scrap trade. The present Lao period of rapid socioeconomic transformation foregrounds desires to transcend these half-century-old battlefields. This book is an examination of the parallel process of remains/revivals in Laos, toward the analysis of the sociocultural aftereffects of war more generally.

My analysis is rooted in the current Lao period of Renovation reforms, a period beginning in the 1990s, after the fall of the Soviet Union, and marked by ongoing socioeconomic liberalization. Contemporary Laos is a single-party socialist state; but increasingly, socialist reforms are loosening, civil groups are forming, and nonstate media are available. The Renovation era in Laos is part of a larger, global post-Soviet transformation that includes the opening of many former Cold War battlefields to Western intervention. The concomitant fall of the Bamboo Curtain (strict border controls around Asia's communist countries, including Laos) also opened Laos to the possibility of hosting international explosive clearance operators, enabling Laos's first explosives clearance programs. Thus, Laos received almost no official postwar aid or clearance assistance until the 1990s, three decades after the war began. The present period of Renovation reforms is also distinguished by a tightening of authoritarian controls, including heightened surveillance, political violence, and forced disappearance. The period of my fieldwork was marked by government harassment targeted against civil society and development workers—just prior to my arrival in the field, Sombath Somphone, a prominent Lao civil society leader, was very publicly disappeared by the police. When I arrived in Laos for primary fieldwork, I found that research agreements I had made prior to Sombath's disappearance required renegotiation; and, fearing the risks of associating themselves with a foreign researcher, one of my host organizations rescinded its patronage altogether. In the final chapter of this book, I analyze my interlocutors' experiences of being "haunted" by Sombath's ghost toward an ethnography of the darker valence of revival—the revival of authoritarianism. This form of state terror functions by making absence visible, a quality that I examine in my elaboration of the haunting of postwar Laos. As these accounts of political violence indicate, the current sociopolitical revival is not limited to strictly liberal practices and includes a revival of authoritarian power and violence. This book is not a linear account of the transition from isolated, war-torn, socialist state to globalizing, peaceful, liberal state; rather, this is an account of the complex and discordant experience of rapid socioeconomic transformation in former battlefields.

Military Waste as Cultural and Area Studies

This book also develops methods, concepts, and theories suited to the complexities and hazards of former battlefields. How might postwar zones constitute their own area studies? Throughout the research and analysis for this book, I found myself drawing on scholarship from diverse war zones: Argentina (Robben 2000), Bosnia (Henig 2012), Cyprus (Navaro-Yashin 2012), Iraq (Daughtry 2015), Korea (Kim 2016), Mozambique (Nordstrom 1997), Sri Lanka (Daniel 1996), Vietnam (Kwon 2008), and Cambodia (Uk 2016), to name just a few. My academic claim, in aligning these studies within this analysis of Laos, is that war zones demand their own cultural and area studies—not as a collection of individual cases, but as a global phenomenon of war and humanitarian intervention that produces its own geographic and cultural formations. I develop a paired approach that treats the study of military waste topically (as one studies courtrooms or schools) and also geographically to the extent that military waste contaminates soils and transforms ecologies, producing an area of shared geographic concern.

This is, essentially, a claim for "metageography" that understands maps as sets of "spatial structures through which people order their knowledge of the world" (Lewis and Wigen 1997, ix). Military waste produces its own cultural and ecological patterns that only partially hew to geopolitical borders, while simultaneously manifesting a durability in the soil that frustrates geopolitical resolution. Military waste has no single front line or battleground, but instead manifests the layering and sedimentation of multiple conflicts over time within the same space. What methods and analytics are best suited to studying this process of layering contamination? The material sedimentation of military waste provokes comparative analysis between conflicts, or across multiple conflicts taken as parts of a single, larger phenomenon. What might be included in a hazardous research methods tool kit for ethnographers studying these zones? In this book, I contribute my own theories and methods to this shared tool kit: a theory of parallelism, whereby war, state violence, and peacetime development are examined in parallel; suggestions for increased subject and researcher protections; and, in particular, a method of poetic attention and field notation (what I call "fieldpoems" and introduce in chapter 1).

This metageographic perspective is partially influenced by Southeast Asian studies. Entanglements of war and scholarship propelled the discipline of Southeast Asian studies into being. This is not to say that Southeast Asia does not exist as an autonomous geographic zone and topic of study (see Benda 1962; Smail 1961); yet in charting this particular conjunction of military and academic processes, I situate this book within a larger geopolitical process that includes the Secret War in Laos. The regional name "Southeast Asia" was itself a political expedient used to refer to the South-East Asia Command during World War II (Anderson 1998; Reid 1993). Later, under the pressures of Soviet and American world building during the Cold War, the idea of Southeast Asia solidified into its present geopolitical and disciplinary shape. The Vietnam-American War intensified the process of forming Southeast Asia as a region and as a discipline: "American anticommunist hegemony created the initial basis for the new field of Southeast Asian studies" present mostly in American universities (Anderson 1998, 8). And yet, Anthony J. S. Reid (1999) asserts that the region did not fully cohere until as recently as the 1990s in partial response to the collapse of the Soviet Union. In Martin W. Lewis and Kären E. Wigen's (1997, 173) view, the coalescing of Southeast Asia during the Cold War was not only a "geopolitical resolution" for purposes of military command, but, importantly, also a "postimperial crisis of spatial conceptualization" resolved, in part, through drawing the bounds of scholarly disciplines. The region and the academic discipline came into being together as a result of ongoing geopolitical intervention. Engaging the ongoing imbrication of war and scholarship, I aim to reverse the logic that cuts up geographic regions as bounded zones of intervention and instead examine the process of intervention itself as a geopolitical, conceptual, and theoretical phenomenon. The nascent disciplinary space that I chart is somewhat prefigured by the international clearance sector, whose practitioners treat military waste as a global problem, addressed via international certification programs, shared methods manuals, standardized data collection practices, and specialized equipment. Evocatively, one clearance operator that I worked with was producing a global map of explosives clearance in which the entire world was mapped onto a massive grid so that every clearance site could be noted in relation to every other clearance site. The whole world prefigured as an explosives clearance zone.

"Military waste" describes the material of war that remains after war has ended. Explosive ordnance in Laos is waste in the sense that these items were abandoned by combatants or failed to detonate during the Vietnam-American War. In Laos, "military waste" broadly applies to military materials such as downed American airplanes and abandoned Russian tanks, the remains of military camps such as helmets and canteens, abandoned and unexploded ordnance such as land mine fields, and the residue of biological weapons such as Agent Orange. These war materials may become waste after a war has ended—and also may become resources as they are repurposed or recycled (airplanes into rebar, bomb cases into cookpots, etc.). How might we theorize this unexpected spoliation of war's remains? International clearance operators treat war remains as ecological contaminants: the use of technical terms such as "contamination," "hazardous area," and "residual risk" give a sense of this ecological approach. This terminology invites analysis of "post-conflict landscapes" (Pholsena and Tappe 2013) as distinct ecological zones, what I present in my work elsewhere as "bomb ecologies" (Zani 2015). In other ways, treating ordnance as waste elides geopolitical conflict to the extent that it naturalizes war and obscures the politics that cuts up battlefields, brackets conflicts, and counts corpses.

While war has inspired significant anthropological theory, the anthropological study of military waste is nascent (Henig 2012; Kim 2016; Uk 2016). Military waste has, to date, generally been taken up as a kind of provocation—something that one encounters in the course of carrying out research on unrelated topics in areas that are contaminated. David Henig (2012), an anthropologist working in Bosnia, developed the term "military waste" to describe the land mines and other ordnance that contaminated his field sites. He did not plan to study military waste, but found that his intended research topic was increasingly terrorized and contaminated by it in a way that compelled his attention. For Henig and other anthropologists studying military waste, the contamination of one's field sites becomes an injunction to study the lived social and cultural impact of explosive ordnance. Eleana Kim (2016), in her pioneering article on military waste in the Korean DMZ, proposes the need for an anthropology of land mines that addresses military waste as a topic of study in and of itself. She theorizes land mine fields in the Korean DMZ as "rogue infrastructure" that provoke unexpected agencies and material possibilities (Kim 2016, 163). Mine fields are rogue in the sense that they embed themselves in an area, offering unexpected alliances and affordances, thereby exceeding imperial geopolitics, ecological expectations, and technological expertise. Mines may be designed as area-denial weapons that limit movement through and use of an area, but people nonetheless interact with them and adapt them for their own purposes. My proposition for treating military waste as area studies resists the conventional logic of clearance, that is, the logic that interprets land mines as contaminants or wastes that are distinct from the context in which they are encountered (as if one could remove them entirely to reveal a prewar culture or environment). Such a discipline would engage the process of wasting itself and examine land mines and other remnants of war as constitutive of contemporary ecological and cultural contexts. Wasting describes an ongoing process of degradation; at the same time, the term gestures toward an afterward beyond violence. Waste exceeds the conditions of its original deployment, provoking new ecological and cultural formations. A scholarship that engages with what war wastes may transcend war and the political claims that bracket conflicts.

The following two sections attend, respectively, to the paired concepts of remains and revivals. The first section presents a brief history of the Vietnam-American War in Laos and the formation of an explosives clearance sector. The second section presents an overlapping history of liberalization, development, and Lao state building. I am, in essence, telling the same story twice in order to introduce my field site. I present these two sections in lieu of a linear history of the war in Laos (see, for example, Coates and Redfern 2013; Jacobs 2012; Kurlantzick 2017). There is value in crafting these historical accounts of war, but there are also other topics worth analyzing in contemporary Laos: ongoing development, peace, and revival may go unaddressed in the course of telling a good war story. My purpose in framing the introduction in this way is to steer clear of overdetermining accounts of the Vietnam-American War and its impact on contemporary Laos. By presenting two overlapping accounts, rather than a single linear account, I foreground my analytic claim for parallelism.

Remains

Remains and revivals together form a paired conceptual frame that I draw upon throughout the book (I discuss revivals in the next section). Both remains and revivals emerged as analytic concepts from my ethnographic research with development organizations and explosives clearance operators in Laos. In the explosives clearance sector, explosive remnants of war is a technical term describing unexploded ordnance (UXO) and abandoned ordnance that remains after a conflict has ended. My use of "remains" references these physical remnants of war as a way of inviting analysis of forms of social life and death that are produced by war and its aftermath. This conceptualization draws on social theories of necropolitics and haunting in which death is analyzed as constitutive of political, social, and economic systems—not destructive or ancillary to such systems (see, for example, Klima 2002; Mbembe 2003). "Remains" carries morbid connotations—the corpse as remains—that I consciously invoke in my use of this term.

The remains/revivals parallel challenges the assumed binarism of life and death that is present, in particular, in new materialism and related social theories of non/human agency. Tempering this trend toward vitalism (see, for example, Bennet 2010; Ingold 2011; Stengers 2012), I ask: How might we theorize agency beyond the abilities of living human (or humanlike) agents? What might a theory of mortalism look like in anthropology? I use the conceptual frame of remains to continually mark the violence of these material and social relations. I analyze how military waste manifests a different kind of agency—one of deathliness—that is a constitutive part of social relations in postwar zones. Explosive ordnance exhibits a form of nonhuman agency that subsists in its own destruction and neglect, whose power increases as human agency recedes: the soldiers die or leave, the planes fly away, and the war ends. Military waste seems, rather, to challenge human agency via its latent power to explode at any time, anywhere. Researching these remains of war, I attend to ethnographic accounts of haunting and ghosts in order to develop a hauntology, or an ontology of military waste as haunting (Derrida 2006; Gordon 2008). I expound this theory at greater detail in chapter 2. In Laos, explosions are commonly described in terms of haunting, where the ghosts of war are said to have triggered explosions, or evil spirits are said to have animated bombs in order to control their detonation. The bombs are "alive," but not in the way that Jane Bennet (2010) uses that term to vivify inanimate objects. Rather, the deadly agency of bombs (to kill, to haunt, to explode) is foregrounded in these ethnographic accounts. My analysis, throughout this book, focuses on this deadly, haunting quality of military waste.

Death may be a means of power, even as it destroys those that are subject to it. Mbembe, in his theorization of necropolitics (after Foucault's theory of biopower as the power to foster or neglect life), refutes the notion that the power to kill only exists in contemporary zones of exception or emergency, such as war zones. Rather, he argues, power may sometimes consist in "*the generalized instrumentalization of human existence and the material destruction of human bodies and populations*" (Mbembe 2003, 14, emphasis in original). I extend this insight to the study of explosives, looking beyond the analysis of military waste as exceptional and instead analyzing how explosive ordnance is, instead, constitutive of a kind of deathly power. I theorize military waste as its own form of power distinct from the intentions of military strategists or the soldiers that emplace minefields or drop bombs—military waste, by definition, persists beyond the conflict of its emplacement. Ordnance is agential via its own destruction. This is not to say that it is purely destructive; rather, and in line with Mbembe's analysis of necropolitics, I am mindfully breaking down the binary that equates life with power and death with passivity and failure, in which the primacy is given to humanlike life. The mortalism of ordnance is distinguished by absence and latency instead of presence and activity. This mortal agency is marked by its own destruction as well as the destruction of its human targets: when a bomb explodes and kills someone, it also destroys itself.

Throughout this book, I carefully use the words "explosive" or "explosion" to describe live ordnance and its detonation. I do this as a political act of linguistic precision, in distinction from the regular practice in explosives clearance and victim assistance of referring to explosions as "accidents" and ordnance as "unexploded ordnance." Where appropriate to a quote, I use the words "accident" or "unexploded ordnance" carefully in context as ethnographic evidence of how explosions are discussed by my interlocutors. The language of explosives clearance leads to peculiar linguistic convolutions, such as a person being the "victim of an unexploded ordnance explosion" whereby a bomb is described as both unexploded and exploded at the same time. These linguistic convolutions are revealing of the necropolitics of military action and victim assistance. As I elaborate in later chapters, talk of accident and unexploded ordnance assumes a misleading divide between war and peace, whereby the end of conflict is assumed to also mark the end of meaningful war violence. Calling an ordnance explosion an accident obscures the intentional violence of war, and of cluster strikes in particular, as part of a long-term process of military wasting. "Accident" implies that each explosion is a singular event, an exceptional misfortune, rather than evidence of how an entire population may be subject to the endemic risks of military waste.

Widespread experiences of risk disrupt the binarism between survivor and victim, abled and disabled, and instead compel analysis of the cultural and political salience of statistically likely injury. Is being in danger a disability?* Drawing on Jasbir K. Puar's (2017) analysis of the necropolitics of debility, the language of the accident disconnects violence from war, obfuscating the political value of debility as an imperial process that extends war. Discussing the general use of the word "accident" to refer to disabling events, Puar writes that "the accident functions as an alibi for the constitutive relations of force [that target specific populations. . . .] Mutilation and amputation are thus no accident but are part of the biopolitical scripting of populations available for injury" (2017, 64). The risks of military waste are not an accidental byproduct of war, but a necessary practice of imperial control; a tactic in and of itself that systematically debilitates target populations far beyond the cessation of conflict. Seen at the level of populations, the end of war may be ancillary to the risks and dangers experienced by target populations over the long term. From this perspective, an accident is not a category of disablement, and certainly not a synonym for civilian casualty or

---

* This project began as a study of victim assistance in Laos, deeply informed by disability studies. As the project and book developed, the focus of my analysis shifted from victim assistance to postwar revival. I think that there is real value in studying these forms of violence while leaving disability somewhat open ended. In instances such as this ("Is being in danger a disability?"), I engage disability in order to disrupt norms of physical impairment and personal misfortune. Engaging disability in this open-ended manner, I have the twofold goal of (1) disrupting the slippage between explosion, survivor, and disabled, whereby the only meaningful impact of an explosion is assumed to be death or disability; and (2) to examine larger ecological and geopolitical processes whose debilitating effects are often glossed as accidental or do not register as direct impairment.

collateral damage; the term, in its very obfuscation, outlines in reverse an important process of widespread endangerment and geopolitical erasure. An explosion is not an accident, and the risks of military waste are not randomly distributed.

The United States covertly bombed Laos in violation of the 1962 Geneva Accords declaring Laos neutral territory during the Vietnam-American War (also known as the Second Indochina War). During this period, from roughly 1964 to 1973, Laos was subject to intense ground battles between communist and royalist factions, especially along the hotly contested Ho Chi Minh Trail that wound through Laos's long, mountainous border with Vietnam and China. This Secret War was simultaneously a revolution, the last major conflict in the protracted Lao wars of independence. This bombing was itself part of a larger Lao civil war between the communist Pathet Lao and royalist factions, lasting from 1959 to 1975, which was itself an extension of the First Indochina War (sometimes known as the Dirty War) against French imperialism beginning in 1946. Additionally, during World War II, Laos had been briefly and violently occupied by the Japanese. To this list, I could also add Thailand's even older occupation of Laos and ongoing skirmishes on the Lao-Thai border. Thus, the 1975 revolution was seen by the Party elites as the final resolution to more than three decades of nearly continuous armed resistance against a succession of foreign imperialists. The Lao nation-state has thus always been contaminated with military waste.

The scale of this Secret War in Laos was unprecedented: it is estimated that the United States covertly dropped more than two million tons of ordnance on Laos.* This amounts to roughly one ton of ordnance for every inhabitant, resulting in at least 30,000 direct casualties (deaths and injuries) during the immediate war years. In total, roughly 200,000 Lao died during the Secret War, representing about one out of every ten persons then living in Laos (Kurlantzick 2017; Stuart-Fox 1997). Additionally, more than a quarter of Laos's population fled as refugees. In the forty years since the war ended, an estimated 20,000 additional casualties have involved the same

---

* This figure does not include ordnance from other combatants, or from ground battles, or ordnance not recorded, or in records that remain classified. I note that the United States is the only combatant in the region to have released records of its involvement in the Secret War. During my fieldwork with explosives clearance teams, I was presented with military waste from a variety of countries, including ordnance from Russia and China.

FIGURE I.2 Cluster submunitions gathered at the base of a tree by bomb technicians during the clearance of this rice field. Photo by the author.

ordnance (Boddington and Bountao 2008). Every province of the country remains contaminated with dangerous live explosives. A half century after war, Laos remains one of the most massively war-contaminated countries in the world. "Massive" is a technical term in the international clearance sector describing contamination over more than 1,000 square kilometers; the category of massive cluster munition contamination was created specifically to describe the unprecedented levels of military waste in contemporary Laos and Vietnam (NPA 2014).

Most of the contamination in contemporary Laos is cluster munitions (see figure I.2). The ordnance in figure I.2 was gathered by a bomb technician during the survey phase of the clearance of a rice field. The technician carefully carried each item of ordnance by hand to the base of this stump in preparation for a controlled demolition. Each item had rusted with time and was now a rough, mottled brown, the ball shrapnel in the casing clearly visible. In Lao, cluster munitions are often called *mee laberd* (bomb mothers) and the cluster submunitions inside called *luk laberd* (bomb children). I first heard these phrases while conducting fieldwork with the explosives clearance team surveying the rice field depicted in figure I.2. An older Lao bomb technician was carefully digging up cluster submunitions with his hands and a small trowel. He called me over and pulled aside a flowering bush to show me the small, rusty sphere of bomb half submerged in the gray soil. "Ni meen luk laberd." Here is a bomb child.

Cluster munitions are usually dropped from aircraft, breaking open in midair to disperse hundreds or thousands of submunitions densely over very large areas. For example, a cluster bomb unit seven (CBU-7) weapons system typically disperses 1,200 ballistic units type eighteen (BLU-18) over roughly 12,000 square meters. An unknown percentage of these units will fail to detonate, as determined by wind and weather conditions, the height from which the munitions were dropped, the quality of the ground (mud), and the accuracy of weapons manufacturing. The Lao government estimates that roughly one-third of the cluster munitions dropped on Laos failed to explode during the bombing (NRA 2010). In the international clearance sector, "cluster munition remnants" refers to unexploded submunitions, failed munitions, and abandoned munitions (NPA 2014, 5). Usually, cluster submunitions, or *bombies* as they are commonly called in Lao, are about twenty kilograms in weight, spherical, and fist sized. They may be painted in a military palate (yellow, brown, green), though, over time, the paint fades and peels to rust. Submunitions that fail to detonate are quite durable and generally do not explode if they are later disturbed or stepped on—but the impact of a hoe or shovel, or the heat of a fire, may detonate them nonetheless.

Walking through a cow pasture that used to be a military camp, and before that a village, a man knelt to collect a handful of dirt. He opened his palm to me, showing the small capsules of pressed black gunpowder leavened into the soil. "Bombs are part of life," he said as he scattered the capsules back into the field, like seeds. He was part of a group of residents that sieved this gunpowder out of the soil in order to resell it on the black market. The bombs, too, were gathered for resale, and were plentiful in the pasture behind us: blue spheres half submerged in the mud; long spike of a rocket visible above the fringe of the grasses; army-green hemispheres difficult to distinguish from rocks underfoot. Thick mist suffused the valley, condensing the colors to a deeper green. A tree grew out of a bomb crater, both perhaps forty years old (figure I.3). The valley was very quiet—there were no cars or

FIGURE I.3 A former Thai military camp converted into a cow pasture near Phonsavan, Xieng Khouang Province. The tree in the foreground is growing out of a large bomb crater. Photo by the author.

electrical appliances in this highland village—and peaceful, strewn with yellow wildflowers. When explosive ordnance becomes endemic, particularly during periods of official peace, ordinary life may manifest a kind of covert violence. Bombs may become "part of life," which is not the same as saying that war becomes ordinary. War and peace, death and life, are not salient binary poles for locating these phenomena; there is a much larger, more complex social field of possible action and experience. The ordnance that remains after the Secret War ended will continue to be explosive for between fifty and 350 years, depending on type and location of emplacement.

Unlike minefields, which are generally too dangerous to farm, cluster-bombed areas are commonly farmed and inhabited. Due to the particular features of this kind of ordnance (small size, durability, and geographic spread), people may live in even very contaminated areas. This capacity to contaminate daily life was designed into the practice of cluster bombing. Analyzing American government reports from the war period, Fred Branfman (2013, 25) demonstrates that a primary goal of the bombing was to destroy the foundations of a viable socialist state if America lost the war. The bombing was intended as a social and cultural intervention at the level of basic, daily life. The ground people walk on; the fields people farm—as my interlocutor said to me in the ethnographic vignette above, "bombs are part of life." The war was never intended to be a conventional military event—it was the first American war to be managed as a covert CIA paramilitary operation, not as a uniformed military operation. In fact, though America technically lost the war in Laos (the state went communist), the operation was considered a success by its American planners. In this view, the war had succeeded in significantly hindering the incoming communist state's capacity to build basic infrastructure and support economic and social systems. Moreover, the Secret War demonstrated that the United States could sustain a long-term conflict with minimal American ground troops and without public or congressional support. Achille Mbembe notes in his theorization of necropolitics that colonial warfare "is not subject to legal or institutional rules. It is not a legally codified activity. . . . Peace is not necessarily the natural outcome of a colonial war. In fact, the distinction between war and peace does not avail" (2003, 25). This logic of intervention does not distinguish between military action and other forms of intervention (including humanitarian assistance). Imperial warfare, rather, perpetuates forms of power via extended, latent violence that permeates daily life.

The success of the Secret War disrupts any simple distinction between war and postwar and, rather, imposes an imperial logic of intervention that exceeds the end of conflict. The war in Laos was a testing ground for a new means of war, including some of the first instances of computer-directed bombing, digital archiving, antipersonnel bombs, aerial gunships, and drone warfare (High, Curran, and Robinson 2013; McCoy 2013). The Secret War became a "template for a new type of large, secret war" that inaugurated the increased global paramilitary involvement of the CIA (Kurlantzick 2017, 16). Alfred W. McCoy goes so far as to argue that the air war in Laos was the "progenitor for warfare in the twenty-first century" (2013, xiv). The Vietnam-American War theater was also an especially potent site, a "critical laboratory" (Redfield 2013, 76) of modern techniques for humanitarian intervention, including the creation of standardized explosives clearance practices. In the half century since the Vietnam-American War, the "Laos model" of warfare (marked by massive aerial bombardment, minimal ground troops, increased collateral damage, and counterinsurgency support via humanitarian assistance) has served as a model for many other conflicts

(Branfman 2013, 30). These sociopolitical forms, including the creation of a paramilitary CIA and of an international humanitarian sector, constitute another part of the Laos model of warfare.*

The Mines Advisory Group (MAG), one of the first major international humanitarian clearance operators, entered Laos in 1994 to begin clearance. In 1989, MAG was founded to help clear the remains of Soviet-era conflicts in Afghanistan. The formation of international humanitarian clearance operators and of an international clearance sector indexes global sociopolitical shifts in the 1990s: as the Soviet Union collapsed, many former Cold War battlefields began opening up to Western humanitarian and developmental intervention. The suffix "humanitarianism," in this period, came to refer to victim-centered forms of care and intervention (Rosenblatt 2015). In the 1990s, the apparatus of war was shifting; the world's first humanitarian clearance operators (MAG, HALO Trust, etc.) were founded in the post-Soviet period by former soldiers choosing to use their skills to clear battlefields rather than fight in them. Humanitarian operators, as opposed to corporate or private operators, work to clear local communities regardless of economic status (though land use does factor into how land is prioritized for clearance) and are not hired privately or paid per area cleared. Today, the international clearance sector is composed of both corporate and humanitarian clearance operators; international organizations that create standards for the sector, notably the Geneva International Centre for Humanitarian Demining, founded in 1998; publications and research in mine action; and international advocacy groups supporting policies for the deployment, stockpiling, and destruction of ordnance. As the most cluster-bombed country in the world, and one of the earliest sites of humanitarian clearance, Laos has become an important testing ground for cluster munition clearance methods.

Bomb technicians that worked in Laos at the start of official clearance described a "ground harvest" of bombs lying so thick on the surface that they could be gathered carefully by hand. A Lao interlocutor in the bomb clearance sector told me that when his family returned to his home village after the war (this was before he worked as a bomb technician), his family discovered a "harvest of bombs" and began gathering them in baskets like fallen fruit. His family collected these bombs at a central point and, when

---

* Laos was not the only testing ground for these new types of counterinsurgency warfare. See Pedersen (2012) on the parallel El Salvador model used in Iraq.

the pile got large enough, lit it on fire from afar—bombs as numerous as fruit, needing to be harvested before they explode. Adding poignant depth to this analogy (bombs as fruit), many kinds of cluster submunitions look like fruits. In Lao, bombs are often called by the names of the fruits they most resemble: a BLU-3 cluster submunition, which is yellow and sits upright upon a flat base, with a large spray of metal fins, is known as a pineapple bomb (*laberd mak nad*). A rocket-propelled grenade, which is long and thin, with a bulbous nose, is known as a cucumber bomb (*laberd mak dtaeng*). And on through the inventory of local fruits and found ordnance (see figure I.2). Another Lao bomb technician once asked me, with all seriousness, whether the American military had studied Lao native fruits in order to design their bombs to "look like fruit, so we will pick them up."

War remains provoke an ongoing, irregular process of social and material ruination: the contamination of the everyday. This process of contamination counters common distinctions between war and postwar—I extend this insight to the broader critique of postcolonial, postconflict, and postsocialist processes, which I return to throughout the book. In analyzing what remains and persists, I draw on recent scholarship of ruins and ruination. Yael Navaro-Yashin, researching postwar Cyprus, uses "ruination" to refer to the "material remains or artifacts of destruction and violation," such as land mines, as well as "to the subjectivities and residual affects that linger . . . in the aftermath of war or violence" (2012, 162). Ruination is an ongoing desolation that matures over time. Ann Laura Stoler (2013, 7), another scholar who attends to the material remains of imperialism, theorizes ruination as "an active, ongoing process that allocates imperial debris differentially," often through the effacement of ruination itself via its erasure from official representation. Military waste contamination creates active ruins that arrest possible futures, especially with regard to postwar reconstruction and development. The ruinous materials in former battlefields are not relics; they are active, corrosive elements of the present and future. The challenge of this kind of scholarship is to understand how violent imperial processes persist in peace, present just beneath the surface of people's lives. My use of mortalism is an elaboration of this scholarly attention toward ruination—my own effort to understand how bombs become part of life. In these former battlefields, deathly agency may work as a counterpolitics to imperialist claims to life and power. As a kind of strategic scholarship, for myself and other scholars, "we look to the lives of those living *in* [ruins]" (Stoler 2013, 15, emphasis in original).

Revivals

Revival is a conceptual frame for analyzing the parallelism of socioeconomic reform, religious awakening, and authoritarian renovation. I use the notion of revivals to invite an analysis of time characterized by resurrections and returns that is inclusive of temporal complexities and pluralities. I am examining a temporal dynamic in which intersecting or layering legacies may produce events that exceed linear cause and effect. Benedict Anderson famously analyzed related experiences of layering temporalities in Southeast Asia as a kind of haunting: linkages to remote events may become so thick as to be disorienting, resulting in a sense of being haunted by the "spectre of comparisons" (1998, 2). Anderson's analysis focuses on the layering process of nation building through colonialism and independence. In the Lao context, the Party state's call for revival is provoked by parallel processes of decolonialization, postwar reconstruction, and liberalization. Additionally, the present revival activates regional cosmologies of state power predicated on moral and temporal cycles in which past, present, and future events coincide.

In 1986, the Lao Communist Party announced a new economic mechanism that opened Laos to nonsocialist sources of aid and investment in a shift toward a market-oriented economy. These ongoing socioeconomic and political reforms are referred to collectively as the Renovation. The Renovation process is extremely fraught, a product of what Grant Evans (1998, 10) identifies as the "serious existential crisis" of the Lao state after the fall of the Soviet Union and weakening of the Communist Brotherhood in Asia in the late 1980s and 1990s. Socialist sources of development aid had begun to dissolve. Shaken by the slow collapse of the Soviet Union, the Lao government's project of socialist construction effectively ended by 1985. By the middle of the 1990s, socialist sources of aid had dwindled to nearly nothing, and by then, Laos had already shifted its base toward liberal funders and models of development (including both private funders and the World Bank). I use "development" to refer to the continuation of particular practices, discourses, and relations between former colonial/imperial powers and former colonies/territories beyond the World War era (Elyachar 2012b). In this book, I use the language of development to examine the particular conjuncture of conflict and reconstruction, or the continuation of relations postconflict. Imbricated in these geopolitical shifts, globally, development in the 1980s more often focused on neoliberal reforms in newly independent states, such as privatizing basic infrastructure (Elyachar 2012b). The forms of aid that predominated in this region after the fall of the Soviet Union often came with social and economic entailments—particular forms of expertise and accountability designed to facilitate the liberalization and decentralization of the Lao Party state.

Throughout these ongoing socioeconomic transformations, the Party sought widespread reform without compromising its single-party leadership. Economic practices previously classified by the Party as neocolonialist, such as the privatization of utilities, were carefully enacted under the guidance of the World Bank and other Western financial and development assistance organizations (Phraxayavong 2009, 135). The post-1985 period of liberalization is the latest in an ongoing effort to create a viable Lao state, characterized by adaptability, rather than by a necessary rupture with socialism. This way of understanding Lao nation building shares traits with classic galactic polity or mandala states (Tambiah 1976; Wolters 1999), as well as being informed by Theravada Buddhist concepts of cyclical time (Hansen 2007). The process of creating a viable Lao state has both temporal and spatial dimensions, manifest through cycles of crisis, destruction, and revival. The total bombing of most major cities and towns during the Secret War unexpectedly accommodates this larger pattern of pulsating urban centers, by turns shrinking and growing. The communist liberation was also a project of urban planning and reform: the creation of cave cities safe from constant bombardment and, after the war, the relocation or reconstruction of bombed-out villages, towns, and cities based upon new, socialist plans. The town of Sepon, a key site of analysis in chapter 2, is one example of a city that was recentered after the war. In its early plans, the new regime was characterized by adaptation rather than rigid dogmatism: in response to the widespread failure of farming cooperatives, collectivization was largely abandoned by 1979, just a few years after the revolution (Askew, Logan, and Long 2006; Evans 1990). Socioeconomic revival and reconstruction were not restricted to the post-Soviet years, but have characterized the Party's ongoing adaptation to the needs of a newly independent but war-ravaged state.

Forty years after the Vietnam-American War ended, development has overtaken any overt process of postwar reconstruction. Laos today receives more foreign aid and financial investment than it has at any other time in its history, surpassing even military assistance and aid to the Royal Lao Government during the Secret War (Phraxayavong 2009, 209). Contemporary

Laos is ranked by the United Nations as one of the least developed countries (LDC) in the world; Laos is also the only such country that has active plans to graduate from that status by 2020 (Cooper 2014). This plan includes a Lao-specific Millennium Development Goal to "Reduce the Impact of UXO" (MDG9). As part of this plan, clearance is currently managed as an aspect of rural poverty alleviation and development—not as an aspect of postwar reconstruction. The clearance sector in Laos is formally managed by the National Authority for UXO/Mine Action. This agency has oversight over explosives clearance, victim assistance, risk education, and national data management and reporting. The clearance sector has been centralized under the purview of the Party state—somewhat notoriously (for my clearance interlocutors) without proper procedures such as audits, anticorruption programs, and financial transparency. Party management of clearance, and the presentation of the Lao state as the victim of bombings, obscures the state's ongoing corruption problems and human rights abuses. There is an essential conundrum at the heart of the clearance sector in Laos: even as the state supports international conventions to ban cluster munitions and land mines, capitalizing on its status as the most bombed country in the world, it is stockpiling antipersonnel mines and has yet to sign the Mine Ban Treaty (LCMM 2017).

In Laos, the language of development also carries additional social and spiritual connotations: development is alternately translated in Lao as either *phattana* or *jaleun*. Both words describe spiritual and material development; in the Lao context, there is no strict division between attaining material prosperity, political influence, and spiritual power. Jaleun, in particular, describes an entity's ability to attain its fullest positive expression, often rendered in terms of attaining enlightenment. The term is tightly linked with spiritual ability (for Buddhists, this means merit-making practices in this life as well as karma from past lives). In recent years, jaleun has become significant due to its association with promises of prosperity and spiritual attainment and its contrast with prior socialist calls for austerity and secularity (Singh 2014). Buddhist rituals that invoke jaleun, such as *basi* ceremonies formerly practiced by the nobility, are now used to bless development projects and otherwise incorporated into the Lao state's exercise of power (Ladwig 2015; Singh 2014). My use of the concept of revival, with its religious connotations in English, is intended to remind the reader of these additional processes of spiritual renewal encoded in development in the Lao context.

In Laos, the development sector consists of international and nongovernmental organizations, local and foreign consultants, local nonprofit associations, mass organizations within the Lao Front for Socialist Construction, government ministries, and village committees. "Nonprofit association" is an official term describing what, in a liberal context, would be called a civil society organization—however, in Lao socialist practice, there is no official distinction between state and civil society. Over this same period, legally recognized religious practices have been broadened and reoriented toward development and economic reform under the control of the Lao Front. Buddhist groups are managed by the government as mass organizations within the Lao Front—Buddhism's official role within the Party state is as an apparatus for socialist, moral education. Elaborating on the religious connotations of phattana and jaleun, I analyze the Lao Sangha (monastic community) and associated groups as part of the Lao development sector. This broader analysis of development derives from my ethnographic data on the overlap between religious and material development and my fieldwork with faith-based development organizations negotiating projects within the Lao Front.

My interlocutors in the development sector told me repeatedly, often accompanied by a shrug of the shoulders or a deep sigh, that "Laos does not have jaleun." Noting a similar refrain among forestry developers, Sarinda Singh writes that while the Lao state is not recognized as having jaleun (an internal capacity for prosperity), "the Lao state is locally perceived as having potential—a power that is yet to be fully realized" (2012, 14). The Lao state's potential for positive transformation is a powerful legitimizer of its political authority, even in the absence of evident successes. The Lao state possesses a latent power: "For the state to have potential, it does not need to be consistently strong, but it does need people to believe that the state has the capacity to provide them with benefits" (Singh 2012, 15). As other scholars of Laos have noted, local political engagement is characterized by extreme ambivalence: colloquial accounts of state corruption and violence are in tension with desires for access, infrastructure, and support (Evans 1990; High 2014; Singh 2014). In Holly High's ethnography of rural development in southern Laos, the state is experienced by locals as "both a potential source of benefit and as a potential source of destruction" (2014, 103). New poverty reduction plans and development programs are often welcomed as evidence of the state's revival, while simultaneously provoking distrust and suspicion among the participants in these programs. High elaborates: "Even when demands for state largess [remain] often unfulfilled, and themselves become the source of disgruntlement, the fantasy remains, and is indeed intensified. The state haunts even those who reject it most forcibly—and this capacity for resurrection and return is one of the key characteristics of desire itself" (2014, 124). Desire for development, desire for progress, occurs in parallel with a haunting sense of corruption and violence. This desire for the state's power to be actualized, rather than latent, has contributed to what High identifies as the "desiring resurrection of the state" (2014, 150). As I describe in chapter 2, these discourses of resurrection often reference a mythical prewar past in which Laos was politically independent, spiritually resolute, and economically prosperous.

Liberalization intensified the new regime's promises of national prosperity: in 1991, at the height of these global and Lao-specific reforms, the Lao state slogan ("Peace, Independence, Unity and Socialism") was amended to include the word "prosperity" (which replaced the word "socialism"). In the same period, the hammer and sickle on the national seal was replaced with the profile of That Luang stupa, commonly recognized as the sacred center of the Lao state (see figure I.4). In these shifts in national symbology, older religious models (coupled with economic reform) replace socialism as the motor of progress. Faith, rather than socialism, appears to sanction the morality of increasing economic prosperity. This practice is in line with a long tradition of Buddhist governance in mainland Southeast Asia (Hansen 2007; Reid 1993; Schober 2010; Tambiah 1984). Speaking generally, scholars have identified Buddhism as the cosmology of the state in mainland Southeast Asia, to the degree that political or economic shifts may be enacted through Buddhist reforms or vice versa (Hansen 2007; Schober 2010). As Reid (1993, 169) reminds us in his now-classic history of Southeast Asia, "all power was spiritual" in this region. Anne R. Hansen (2007), studying Buddhist modernism in colonial and postcolonial Cambodia, understands modern state reforms as part of a long tradition of Buddhist purification or renewal. Sociopolitical shifts may present as the erosion of religious systems, requiring moral revival and reform. In Buddhist cosmology, moral progress necessarily manifests different kinds of worlds through time. More specifically, "the corporeality of the world, its inhabitants, and its temporal cycles are tied to the moral behavior of human beings" (Hansen 2007, 22). Reforms are a natural and inevitable part of how people respond to change, and manifest change, in a world that is always in process. Contra reform, continuity in this cosmology is something that has to be worked for "through

FIGURE I.4 That Luang stupa receiving offerings during the yearly
festival in its honor. Photo by the author.

the replication and renewal of earlier forms" (Tambiah 1984, 240). Things
do not endure; continuity is achievable only through replication or renewal.

These religious concepts of sovereignty and revival were never completely effaced: significantly, the 1975 liberation was officially celebrated via
a Party march to That Luang; and the yearly That Luang festival (to ritually support the prosperity of the state) was permitted by the Party even in
the early years of intense socialist reform (Askew, Logan, and Long 2007;
Ladwig 2015). Analyzed within this larger cosmology of spiritual renewal,
the present revival appears as just the latest in a long cycle of spiritual and
material development. In this kind of cyclical time, the old and the new may
sometimes switch places: socialist regulations governing comportment and
dress are loosening, and Buddhist rituals (associated with the monarchy) are
now often practiced by government officials and even Party members (Evans
1998). People are now often wearing older styles of clothing associated with
the monarchy, especially the *sihn*, or ethnic Lao skirt. Yet the choice to revive
older practices has come to point to a "future imagined modernity, not to the
past" (Evans 1998, 87). In spite of these renewed promises of wealth via social and spiritual renewal, and partly due to its new economic entanglement

with Thailand, Laos was extremely hard hit by the 1997 Asian financial crisis and 2008 global mortgage crisis. The present Renovation era carries this additional charge, a potentiality after crisis or between past and future crises.

Methodological Frame

This four-year field research project began in 2012 and ended in 2015, involving a total of seventeen months of ethnographic fieldwork in Laos. My primary research site was Vientiane, the capital of Laos, where I was hosted primarily by an explosives clearance operator (2012–13) and a faith-based development organization (2014–15). Beyond the capital, I spent significant time conducting fieldwork with development organizations and explosive clearance teams from four different operators in four provinces of the country: in the far north, Xieng Khouang Province, original stronghold of the communist Pathet Lao revolutionaries and site of the secret city of Long Tieng, an airbase from which the CIA managed its covert bombings; Khammouane Province, mostly forested and mountainous; Savannakhet Province, whose name means City of Paradise, a former royal capital and colonial capital; and, to the far south, Salavan Province, stretched across the agriculturally fertile Bolaven Plateau. These provinces are the most contaminated parts of Laos. I also conducted trips to Champasak Province, Luang Namtha Province, and Luang Prabang Province.

My fieldwork was characterized by learning how to perceive what is only unevenly perceivable, or layered beneath what is overtly perceivable. This was largely a challenge inherent to studying military waste a half century after war—ethnographic evidence almost necessarily consists of traces, ghosts, remains. "Remains," here, is also a methodological concept. The constitutive parts of my fieldwork praxis acquired surreal, often sinister, qualities. "Evidence," for example, is a technical term in the explosives clearance sector for data used to determine if clearance is necessary in a particular area. A bomb is evidence. A crater is evidence. Evidence often explodes, destroying itself and the person who found it. A death is evidence. This adjustment of fieldwork praxis has been remarked upon by other ethnographers in their own studies of violence. E. V. Daniel, in his work on political violence in Sri Lanka, writes, "The very words 'project,' 'informants,' 'information,' 'interview,' 'evidence,' 'description' took on new and terrifying meanings" (1996, 3). The methodological and theoretical praxis for his research were in "a state of utter discordance that [was] sustained by the relentless presence—now exploding, now simmering—of violence" (3). But whereas Daniel experienced a terrorizing of seemingly normal parts of his research (an interview, a project), I experienced the normalization of terror in my field site. Daily life and war violence merge such that the violence is no longer exceptional. In this shaping of the everyday by military waste, it becomes difficult to hold on to the terror of violence—cluster bombs contaminate people's everyday lives, becoming just one among many risks and resources for people inhabiting these often rural and impoverished parts of Laos. This experience of having my research methods terrorized by war is part of my development of hazardous research methods as outlined in chapter 1.

Military waste is perceivable only from certain vantage points, a quality that bomb technicians calculate in order to occupy positions of safety on the margins of controlled demolitions. I examine this phenomenon, as it relates to the sound of explosions, in chapter 3, where I explore the process of learning to listen from the margins of explosions. In the course of this research, I actively engaged my interlocutors in learning to perceive remains of war. One of these interlocutors, a bomb technician, and I would play a guessing game: "Is it a crater or a hole?" One of us would point out a hole in the ground and the other would guess whether it was a bomb crater—and had to justify the answer with evidence. Holes that drew our attention might variously include watering holes, buffalo ponds, fish farms, trash pits, fire pits, and drainage caches. My interlocutor, for example, might point out that there was a small lip of debris around the rim of a fish pond, indicating that the hole was probably produced by an explosion. The ability to correctly identify craters and holes was an important part of clearance survey practices; during the survey stage, craters were evidence used to determine if an area was contaminated. Additionally, correctly identifying craters was an important way to manage one's own safety in an area that might or might not be contaminated.

This unsettling sensibility—learning to recognize the traces of war—contaminated my fieldwork even when I was not working directly in a clearance zone. A visit to an interlocutor's home village in rural Savannakhet stands out as formative of this experience. While staying with my interlocutor's family, I regularly accompanied her when she escorted the family's buffalo from morning pasture to evening pasture. The pastures were situated around many circular ponds in which the buffalo sat with supreme contentment. My memories of this village were similarly suffused with feelings of comfort and ease. Later, when I was taking a plane back to Vientiane, the plane happened to take a route that flew over this same village. We were flying low enough to the ground that I could distinguish the features of the recognizable houses, pastures, and footpaths of my interlocutor's home. It occurred to me: this is what villages look like to bomber pilots. And from that height, I could recognize that the large ponds in the pastures were actually arranged in a bomb strike pattern. They were bomb craters, not only ponds. Conducting this research well required that I learn how to switch between points of view, learning to see from the ground as easily as from the air. Those bomb ponds, like many ghostly traces of war, were difficult to perceive directly from any single position. This perceptual switching was tempered by a sense of elision, or misdirection, akin to looking for an optical illusion in a holographic image.

Ethnographic reorientations such as these invite a discussion of the politics of perception in fieldwork. Accounts of ethnographic methods for studying war and violence have focused on questions of representation (Daniel 1996; Nordstrom 2004). I was much more vexed by questions of perception. There seemed to be a major disjuncture between the mode of empiricism I had been taught as an ethnographer (one premised on lived, everyday experience) and the surreal experiences of myself and my interlocutors inhabiting these zones of military waste. I use the word "surreal" to indicate the experience of layering realities, by which the everyday is punctuated by latent danger lying beneath and lingering into the future. The very material of everyday life seemed to be contaminated in a way that resisted my awareness. I had to learn to perceive military waste, even though it was right there beneath my feet. How do I perceive and study this subtle subterranean violence, with all its complex and unintended effects, and also study those presently living just above it?

Learning to carry out this fieldwork and interpret my field data meant increasing my capacity to dwell in "nonknowing," which I experienced in Laos primarily as a sense of perpetual secrecy and paranoia (after Agamben; see Jackson 2013, 153). In my ethnographic practice, I cultivated "knowledge about absence," where "loss of knowledge [was treated] as part of the data, not as loss of the data" (Strathern 2004, 97–98). I found that this research frustrated my every effort at "thick description," which I understood as a mode of theory and representation rooted in the disclosure of cultural context, meaning, and depth (Geertz 1973). The very act of cultural disclosure became untenable, particularly as I sought to deflect frequent accusations that I was a spy or that my research was unsafe because I was being spied on.

The injunction to keep things secret and private constituted a crucial quality of my ethnographic data, compelling methods and modes of representation attentive to silence and uncertainty. These methodological and ethical struggles had the unexpected consequence of troubling my assumptions about the act of ethnography, particularly as a practice of empirical research and writing. Critically engaging with conventions in ethnographic writing toward the "fetishization of thickness" (Jackson 2013, 152), I examine modes of writing premised on thin description and related ethical and representational responses (Jackson 2013; Love 2013; Simpson 2014). Thinness and thickness are parallel representational practices in that they exist in generative tension, without necessarily converging or contradicting each other. My use of thin description is not a rejection of the Geertzian model of thick description, but is a related representational practice rooted in the particularities of my field site (such as my interlocutors' paranoia and reticence to speak). I strive to accurately describe the thinness of my data and respect my interlocutors' choices for nondisclosure (where thinness is, itself, a form of ethnographic evidence).

Clifford Geertz asserts that "ethnography is thick description and ethnographers are those who are doing the describing" (1973, 16). Yet even as he propounds an interpretive method of thickness, Geertz is careful to warn that "cultural analysis is intrinsically incomplete" (29). He writes that "coherence cannot be the major test of validity for a cultural description. . . . The force of our interpretations cannot rest, as they are now so often made to do, on the tightness with which they hold together, or the assurance with which they are argued" (17). One of Geertz's examples of comparable interpretive rigor is the act of interpreting a poem, in which the reading of the poem includes an explication of the interpretive logic of the poet and the poem's readers: who wrote the poem, who reads the poem, and what meanings the poem evokes for readers (rather than simply counting its lines and syllables). The goal is not analytic totality, the presumption of seeing or understanding everything; an interpretation has succeeded when it evokes the imaginative universe that imbues poems with meaning for poets and readers alike. In chapter 1, I examine my own use of poetry as a field method for recording and analyzing complexity and contradiction.

This approach to ethnographic fieldwork follows a tradition in feminist anthropology of cultivating "partial knowledge" as a tonic against modes of knowledge production that assume privileged total access to phenomena (Strathern 2004). I adapt parallelism as a methodological concept in this book in the manner of feminist theories that root methods in lived, embodied experiences of struggle. Turning to Sara Ahmed's use of sweaty concepts: "Sweat is bodily; we might sweat more during more strenuous and muscular activity. A sweaty concept might come out of a bodily experience that is trying. The task is to stay with the difficulty, to keep exploring and exposing this difficulty" (2017, 13). My methods are inspired by the very real challenges of carrying out fieldwork in a repressive, authoritarian country with a record of human rights abuse, where I and my interlocutors were subject to ongoing government surveillance and threat. With this kind of knowledge, as for many kinds of qualitative data, certainty and completeness cannot be the rubric for success. Instead, there is an impulse to wrangle with the qualities of knowledge itself (and of knowledge production) as an ethnographic process that involves interactions with one's informants. An interlocutor's or researcher's choices to not disclose details of a story are an important aspect of research ethics: these moments of "ethnographic refusal" (Simpson 2014) are poignant encounters with the personal stakes of research and representation—and opportunities to carefully assess research practices. Carrying out this fieldwork provoked me to reassess the methods/ethics framework in ethnography; my use of parallelism as a framing concept emerged from this careful reassessment. Parallelism is not a concept that facilitates resolution—it is a concept of ongoing struggle, irresolution, and incompleteness. As I describe in chapter 1, parallelism became a crucial method of attention to the unsaid, silenced, or contradictory. My response to these methodological and ethical challenges was to preserve the incompleteness of my data, in some cases by examining gaps in data or, in other cases, by purposefully obscuring details of my interlocutors' lives. There is thus a parity between my experiences of carrying out this research and my analytic framing of the book: I preserve the sense of struggle and absence within my writing.

As a consequence of my careful attention to these methodological and ethical concerns, I have chosen to eschew standard anonymization practices that replace subject identifiers with composite characters or fake identifiers. None of my interlocutors are identified by name, and only the most minimal details of their lives are presented to the reader. I carefully present uncertainties in my ethnographic data and maintain disrupted narratives as constitutive of my ethnographic analysis. Where appropriate to my argument, I may mark that an interlocutor is recurring from a previous chapter, but, in general, I also eschew creating narrative arcs for specific, recurring interlocutors. This partially replicates my field notation practices, in which I assigned interlocutors code names in the field (that could be decoded later using a cipher that I memorized) and thus never included actual names in my field notes. "Thin description is soaked in purposeful cover-ups, nonrevelations, and calculated glosses. . . . So, there are secrets you keep. That you treat very preciously. Names of research subjects you share but many more you do not. There is information veiled for the sake of story. For the sake of much more" (Jackson 2013, 153). The reader's sense of incompleteness is intentional; I am replicating, in my writing choices, the qualia of paranoia and secrecy that characterized my ethnographic data. A representational practice of thinness and partiality is not a license to write anything, any which way I choose without regard to validity. For kinds of data that are silenced or ghostly, direct disclosure or overly zealous fact checking may counter the aim of research; there are many kinds of ethnographic data for which existential questions of truth or objectivity are simply beside the point. I am not rejecting conventional modes of ethnographic writing, but rather pursuing shared goals of humility, respect, and care toward the interlocutors and the communities I study.

In format, my book performs its own response to these concerns: the chapters of this book are arranged to provoke parallel readings, for example, through the repetition of topics across chapters; and within each chapter, I juxtapose individual sections and employ / marks to bring parallels to the reader's attention (such as the remains/revivals parallel). The reader will find poems as interleaves between each chapter of the book (the first is just prior to this introduction). This is designed to create a sense of parallel reading: one may read the poems as standalone pieces, in the interleaves, without theorization or critique; or one may read, in the chapters themselves or in the appendix, the poems as analytic entities subject to explanation. My use of poetry plays with the idea of ethnographic data in a text—a playful nod to Geertz's (1983, 70) famous assertion that learning the "natives' inner lives" is very like learning to properly "read a poem," where cultures are approached analytically as texts. The reader's process of interpreting these poems is expressive of my fieldwork experience; an experience of interpretive uncertainty that was very present in my ethnographic data. This builds toward my larger claim that narrative language does not have a monopoly on truth, or more pointedly, on representing field data. Some field data are best recorded as narrative notes; other data as poems (Faulkner 2009); others as drawings (Taussig 2011); others as audio recordings (Feld 2012), and so on.

I assert that, as anthropologists, the heterogeneity of our field data compels us to acquire more flexibility (and playfulness) in our data collection and representation practices. This book is one, among many, interventions in the field that presents nonnarrative forms of scholarship alongside more conventional narrative scholarship.

Chapter Overview

The book begins with a chapter on parallelism and proceeds through three ethnographic chapters that each explores a different aspect of remains/revivals in contemporary Laos. In chapter 1, "The Dragon and the River," I present an argument for parallelism as a method of ethnographic attention and as ethnographic evidence for contemporary Lao politics. This chapter introduces my primary field sites and fieldwork relations with development organizations and clearance operators, and, via an examination of authoritarianism and the culture of paranoia in Laos, also foregrounds contemporary dangers of the lingering remains of a half-century-old war. The title of the chapter refers to a simple parallel: the government has outlawed swimming in the river because the water dragon is dangerous and the river current is dangerous. The two statements express a tension in Lao politics wherein the current secular socialist regime cannot officially recognize the dragon's traditional, religious claims to sovereignty and violence. Spurred by the challenges of carrying out fieldwork in an authoritarian socialist country, I examine Laos's culture of paranoia as ethnographic evidence of authoritarian revival and as incitement to methodological innovation. I draw on ethnographic examples of Lao poetic parallelism to develop a method of poetic inquiry, what I term "fieldpoems," for hazardous fieldwork.

In chapter 2, "Ghost Mine," I examine the haunting of Sepon, an industrial center in the mountains of Savannakhet. Sepon is both the home of Laos's first gold mine (the centerpiece of the state's economic liberalization plan) and one of the most war-contaminated zones in the country. Based on fieldwork with explosives clearance teams in Sepon and interviews with workers at the gold mine, I examine the fraught resurrection of the state at the Sepon Gold Mine (High 2014). Workers at the mine are unearthing gold, copper, explosive bombs, archaeological artifacts, and ghosts that possess mine workers. The gold mine is also a ghost mine: a place where one unearths ghosts or becomes a ghost oneself. I analyze parallel accounts of the gold mine and ghost mine to develop a hauntology of military waste in Laos.

In chapter 3, "Blast Radius," I use the sound of an explosion as my entrance into an analysis of endangerment and embodiment in contaminated zones. I analyze this sound within a Lao cosmology of resonant power. A bomb that explodes within this field of force has a sociopolitical and spiritual blast radius. People inhabit this blast radius as a zone of disabling possibility—whether or not they are directly injured by the blast. Turning to the resonant power of other sounds within this cosmology, I contrast the sound of a bomb going off with the sound of chanted poetry used by Buddhist monks during mine risk education trainings.

In the conclusion, "Phaseout," I reflect on the ending of my fieldwork and the concomitant phaseout of a major development organization that hosted part of my research. This organization's exit from Laos was compelled, in part, by the forced disappearance of Sombath Somphone, a high-profile Lao aid worker. To explain the haunting of Laos's present revival, I analyze the forced disappearance of Sombath and his ghost's subsequent haunting of the Lao development sector. I compare this phaseout with my own ambivalent entrance/exit to fieldwork in Laos. I use this account of the haunting of Lao development to summarize the process of remains/revivals in contemporary Laos. I use these accounts of disappearance and phaseout to examine the stakes in developing a hazardous research methods tool kit and to extend an invitation to future work on the anthropology of military waste. My reflection on exits, phaseouts, and disappearances appropriately concludes the book.

FIELDPOEM 11
The Fruit Eaters

The exceedingly virtuous eat only fruit that freely falls
without knowledge of death

She forages from the forest:
cucumber bombs
guava bombs
bael bombs
pineapple bombs
melon bombs

"Sometimes I wonder if they
are supposed to look like fruit
so that we will pick them up."

She holds a yellow bomb the size of her fist
with fins like the blades of pineapples

1 • THE DRAGON AND THE RIVER

Learning to Think in Two Ways

After the monsoon rains, regular as clockwork every afternoon, I stopped by a friend's shop for tea and conversation. Her shop was a few blocks from the Mekong River in downtown Vientiane, the capital of Laos. Along this part of the riverfront, preparations were under way for the Boat Racing Festival to honor and entertain the *naga*, or water dragons, that live in the river. Historically, naga have been keepers of civil order in Mekong cities (Askew, Logan, and Long 2007). Naga sanction laws, adjudicate conflicts, appoint rulers, and devour wrongdoers. A naga is content when the government is prosperous, lawful, and devout. If the government is weak or immoral, naga may show their displeasure by rampaging through riverside communities. Over tea, my friend wistfully commented that people used to be able to swim safely in the river. When she was a child, she told me, people were respectful and made offerings to the Vientiane naga. Swimming fatalities were rare. Recently, however, there had been several prominent fatalities. The local government has banned swimming—even during the festival in the naga's honor.

"So is the naga killing people and that is why swimming is illegal?"

She slowly shakes her head to one side and then the other, equivocating, then looks me squarely in the eyes: "Leah, you must learn that the Lao think in two ways: the naga in the river *and* we don't know how deep it is."

Hearing the hardening of her tone of voice, I got a feeling of crossing deep waters myself. I sat in the silence after her statement, waiting for further clarification, which she did not provide. We were alone; there was no one else present to critique her remark, yet she spoke as if she was afraid. I recalled another conversation I had with this friend: she had pointed at the seedpods of a tree growing in front of her shop, the seeds like lapping green tongues as long as my arm, known in Lao as tree tongues (*lin mai*), and remarked, "Be careful. In Laos, even the trees have tongues."

Vientiane was under curfew; it was common to see soldiers on patrol or at checkpoints at major intersections, though there were none visible from our seats on the porch of her shop. I sipped my bael-fruit tea and thought. She made no effort to reconcile the dangerous naga and the dangerous river, or to explain whether the government was afraid of the righteous anger of a Vientiane naga. My feeling was that the tension between her parallel statements, the ability to "think in two ways," was the meat of her remark: the government wanted to protect its people from the currents of a monsoon-swollen river, and the government wanted to prevent the local naga from devouring people, implying the regime's weakness. Simultaneously, the government, nominally socialist and secular, would not publicly admit the naga's existence. It was not merely that my question was simplistic. Rather, my assumption that there would only be one answer prevented me from appreciating crucial complexities of Lao politics and culture in a period of socialist reform, economic liberalization, and religious revival. My friend tried to teach me this lesson very early on in my fieldwork, but it was not until I became more familiar with Lao politics and the Lao language that I learned to follow her advice and think in two ways.

This chapter is inspired by this first encounter with ethnographic data in the form of parallels, though my argument is not limited to a discussion of the dragon and the river. As my Lao language skills improved, I came to recognize my friend's statement as an example of a common Lao way of expressing information in two ways simultaneously: poetic parallelism. Parallelism is a creative style or poetic form in which statements are juxtaposed, often through the repetition of similar sounds, grammars, structures, or themes. Parallels develop their richness from the latent equivalencies between everyday concepts; speakers draw on a shared pool of poetic references and current events to create subtle, textured parallels. The form has attracted scholarly attention for its potential to "provide insight into what the poets and their audiences themselves intuitively consider to be the most interesting equivalents" (Keane 1997, 107).* My argument is not that parallelism is a unique Lao way of thinking, nor am I arguing that it is a special adaptation to life under socialist regimes. Parallelism is a common poetic practice throughout Southeast Asia, predating the current Lao Party state. Nor does parallelism necessarily take the form of poems, though poetry is central to its cultural enactment in Laos. Parallelism has its roots in spoken Lao and is not limited to strict poetic forms. Simple parallels were commonly used in conversations among my friends and colleagues to craft nuanced jokes, express complex opinions, and share hazardous information.

I engage parallelism in the field as provocation to methodological reflection and innovation. In this sense, this chapter is about parallelism as a quality of hazardous research and not about Laos or Lao poetic parallelism, though it is rooted in the specific Lao hazards of surveillance, police harassment, self-censorship, and lingering war violence. I employ the term "hazard" as a broad conceptual frame that includes hazards encountered in the field, such as war violence, and hazardous research methods that engage these hazards as a means of anthropological knowledge production. All anthropologists deal with hazards in fieldwork to the extent that hazards significantly shape the human experience. How should we protect ourselves and our research subjects when we work in hazardous field sites? How should we ethically carry out research with people whose daily practices and utterances are inflected with extreme paranoia? How might we learn to hear what is not speakable? As I discuss in this chapter, parallelism became a crucial mode of engaging these methodological and ethical concerns, while also being an important component of my data on postwar Laos. The surveillance paranoia that I analyze in this chapter constitutes only one possible type of research hazard, and poetic parallelism constitutes only one possible methodological response. In an authoritarian context marked by state surveillance and the threat of violence, the very form of the parallels enacts

---

* The form has attracted more theoretical attention than ethnographic attention (see, for example, Jakobson 1966). In this chapter, I draw on Peter Koret's (1999, 2000) pioneering work on Lao parallelism as a literary tradition (he does not treat it as ethnographic evidence). For another ethnographic account of parallelism in Southeast Asia, see James Fox's (1971, 1974) ethnography of Roti ritual language in eastern Indonesia.

relations and is itself data on Lao society. It is these linkages between poetry, paranoia, and hazardous research that I analyze in this chapter.

Postwar revival and development are challenging, politically sensitive topics to research even under the best of circumstances. The People's Democratic Republic of Laos is an authoritarian, repressive regime, born of revolution and warfare. The surveillance paranoia that I analyze in this chapter is one component of a larger Lao culture of terror that includes secret prison camps, forced resettlement, and political disappearance (Taussig 1987; see the conclusion for an extended discussion). "Cultures of terror" refers to sociopolitical systems in which "order . . . is maintained by the permanent, massive, and systematic use or threat of violence and intimidation by the state" against its own population, for whom "fear becomes a way of life" (Sluka 2000, 22–23). For example, my friend's comment that "even the trees have tongues" is efficacious, as a kind of paranoia rooted in state terror, regardless of the state's actual capacity to wiretap and conduct surveillance. While specific instances of surveillance may be implausible, this paranoia is supported by an authoritarian sociopolitical context characterized by the pervasive use of violence and threat.

My fieldwork experiences imply a parallelism as method: My friend's skill at delicately describing the stakes in swimming in the river prompted me to consider my own ability to research hazardous topics. I offer parallelism as a conceptual frame for understanding hazards in ethnographic fieldwork and anthropological knowledge production. This approach reflects my slow sensitization to the hazards of fieldwork in Laos. My preliminary fieldwork plan for this research assumed I would encounter obstacles (for example, my ethics protocols and other research subject protections assumed I would be targeted for government surveillance). Yet there was no way for me to predict the specific challenges, or the cultural richness of these challenges, prior to entering this field site. My fieldwork experiences of paranoia compel me to align my analysis of parallelism with the analysis of the sociocultural context that makes information hazardous. While the ethnographic accounts that I present in this chapter come from both urban and rural contexts across three provinces of Laos, they each occurred in spaces of interaction between Lao and foreigners: local headquarters of foreign organizations, program sites for development projects, shops and cafés popular with both locals and foreigners. These are spaces of interaction, but also spaces of surveillance and control. The capital, Vientiane, with its special openness to foreigners, was particularly marked by surveillance, curfew, police checkpoints, and the like. This chapter moves through a parallelism of its own, in that it lies at the nexus of anthropological debates regarding the ethnography of violence and war (see, for example, Daniel 1996; Nordstrom 1997) and the hazards latent in ethnographic intimacy (see High 2011). My analysis engages these discipline-level discussions while being rooted in my ethnography of authoritarian power in contemporary Laos.

I employ parallelism as a means of consciously reorienting myself, seeking other perspectives that enrich my research and analysis. My focus in this chapter on cultures of paranoia works to foreground contemporary experiences of state terror, setting ongoing war violence into the background—and into later chapters in the book. Arranging in this manner, my aim is to firmly root my study of war's aftereffects in a discussion of contemporary Lao culture and sociopolitics. Hazards may layer upon each other without being wholly commensurable. In the next section, I introduce Lao poetic parallelism as a method for presenting multiple statements simultaneously, inviting or foreclosing multiple readings. Understanding the features of parallels enables my analysis, in the later sections of this chapter, of my own and my interlocutors' surveillance paranoia and the sociopolitical context that supported our paranoia. I engage prevalent surveillance paranoia as fieldwork dilemmas requiring an ethical response and as data for an ethnography of the Lao state. In the final section, I turn again to poetic parallelism to analyze my use of fieldpoetry as a methodological and ethical response to experiences of hazard in fieldwork.

Lao Parallelism in Poetry and Practice

The poetic form that I examine in this chapter was codified in the twentieth century as part of nationalist efforts to identify specifically Lao literature. The standardization of poems into two hemistichs, or distichs (split lines across parallel columns of the poem) occurred as recently as the 1990s—a process culminating in what Peter Koret describes as the "reinvention of Lao literature" (1999, 238). New poetic styles, authorized by the Ministry of Education, were taught in schools as a traditional Lao literary style. My interlocutors identified poetic parallelism as a traditional and Buddhist form, without recognizing its very recent standardization. The Lao form of parallelism is also commonly found in northeast Thailand, and more broadly among non-Lao ethnicities within mainland Southeast Asia (Koret 1999).

Parallelism is a form of creativity with roots in the spoken Lao language. It is, after Roman Jakobson's (1966, 403) pioneering theorization of the form, a kind of "pervasive parallelism" that activates interrelated domains of oral language, written language, and everyday cultural practice. Written distichs replicate spoken parallels, repeating themes, words, and tones as well as the use of assonance, alliteration, consonance, and silence. Most written Lao poems are likely to have originally existed as multiple, simultaneously circulating, oral versions (Koret 2000). When transcribed, poems are often written on perishable leaves or paper, requiring regular recopying for preservation and circulation. When a poem is recopied, it is frequently changed by the copier (generally a young monk). Poems rarely carry the name of an author, and under these circumstances of frequent and expected amendments, identifying a single author would miss the point. The poems do not have single authors. The content of poems follows a similar logic: topics, characters, themes, even lines or phrases are not considered the invention of a singular poet. Poets draw on a shared collection of poetic resources to craft poems; the skill is in the clever juxtaposition of known content rather than in the creation of new content. Koret elaborates, "To understand Lao literature and the nature of its composition, it is necessary to reconcile two conflicting statements, that individual Lao stories have multiple authorship and that they have no author at all. According to traditional Lao belief, the stories that comprise Lao literature are taken from Buddhist religious sources rather than being the creation of the Lao themselves. The literature's perceived religious origin . . . makes the concept of literary authorship appear sacrilegious if not irrelevant" (2000, 210). In this fashion, poetry recapitulates the "this-worldly/otherworldly parallelism" that scholars have identified in Lao–Theravada Buddhist cosmology more generally (Holt 2009, 39). This-worldly forms, whether poetical or political, are understood to exist in dynamic relation with the otherworlds of deities and spirits. The person who writes the poem does not consider themselves to be the poem's original creator, but sits at some distance from the poem understood as an inspired, semiautonomous entity.

This doubling effect is most clearly visible in the form of the poems themselves: a typical Lao poem is written as a set of two to four distinct columns. One reads across the distich, letting the gaps between columns enhance the resonance of the parallels. The center-most two columns contain the core content, with the outermost columns providing peripheral information on setting, time period, or speaker. Below, I've included the first two stanzas of a modern poem written by a group of development monks, so called for their participation in development projects, for a mine risk education project managed by an international nongovernmental organization. Figure 1.1

shows a group of young novices going through risk education materials as they brainstorm appropriate sermons. The full poem is a Buddhist sermon, designed to be memorized and recited at religious events. The full poem includes sections on the danger of tampering with bombs, how to offer spiritual support to victims, and the importance of honoring disabled family members. I have kept the distich in my English version, though the norm is to remove it in translation, in order to preserve the crucial sense of distance between distichs. I transcribed the poem in phonetic Lao so that the sonic register of the parallels is more obvious (but for the sake of simplicity, I have chosen not to notate tones).

Thaan thii maa jaak gkaam	daen daan din dai gaw dii
Thook thua thang logka	phaen phuum phai pheuun
Yoo ahsii leuu ahfrika nan	europ odsadaalii
Hed haa tii soi gkuu	phai haai manud khon

Honorable people from far-	away lands
All together the world	underneath the plains, mountains
Within Asia or Africa	Europe or Australia
Make us worthy to clear	dangerous bombs

In the original Lao, each part of the poem is itself made up of smaller parallels. The phrase "faraway lands" is split across the distich, such that the gap creates a sense of farness. The first line is split between the first half, marked by the repetition of the *th* consonant, and the last half, marked by the repetition of the long *aa* vowel. Within each half of the line, the sound repetitions create additional internal parallels between words (*thaan thii*, for example). These paired sounds, in turn, resonate with the repetition of similar sounds or tones elsewhere in the poem. These examples of internal parallels elucidate three features of Lao poetry: first, that parallelism is a creative practice present at every scale of the poem, and not merely a poetic form; second, that paired entities are equivalent, but not identical. This is repetition with difference, each time. There is no assumption of allegiance or fidelity to an original. And third, pairs are not singular, but are often multiply paired to other parts of the poem. One has the sense of emergent, multiplying pairs, rather than an overarching system of poetic construction. Like Jakobson, in his analysis of parallels, I find that when the poems are subjected to analysis, they do not yield to simplicity but rather reveal "a network of multifarious compelling affinities" in which each line "is indissolubly interlaced with the

FIGURE 1.1 Buddhist monks and novices developing religious sermons about mine risk education at a training in Phonsavan, Xieng Khouang Province. Photo by the author.

near and distant verbal environment" (1966, 429). But, as with the parallels themselves, these connections do not require or assume a hegemonic status. There is no easy isomorphism between these poems and Lao cosmopolitical "doubling." The poems elude such easy equivalents and in this way resist the formation of large-scale systems or theories, as well as individual authorship. Recall, there is no author; the poems are written by no one and everyone at the same time. It is important to me, as a scholar, that my ethnography maintain this sense of incompleteness and frustrated origins. I am consciously choosing not to reify a cohesive system. The power of parallels is in the friction, or juxtaposition, of things that seem like they should be the same, or should sound the same, but somehow do not.

When I initially translated this poem with one of my Lao tutors, I asked him if it was intentional that Asia and Africa were in one column, and Europe and Australia were in the other. I read an intimation of socioeconomic classes, where the bombs were associated with richer, Western countries ("Europe or Australia/dangerous bombs"). And America, the source of most of the bombs, is pointedly not listed among the "honorable people."

He quickly cautioned me, "You could do that, but we must not read like that! If you read like that, it might make someone unhappy, so it is important that we just read across the columns." Quite literally, the distichs in a poem may be read across or down. Some poems are intentionally written so that alternate meanings emerge horizontally or vertically. My tutor's words reflected his concern with teaching me proper knowledge, but his tone of voice implied that an improper reading was certainly possible, perhaps more so for me than for him ("*You* could do that, but *we* must not"). His caution highlighted for me the hazards in reading poems one way over another. Part of learning how to read parallels is learning the difference between a proper and an improper reading. Parallels have the power to invoke dangerous equivalents that may remain unvoiced, latent, within the poem.

The parallel form may be as small as paired words (*thaan tii*) or paired hemistichs ("faraway lands"), or as large as an entire section, a complete poem, or an entire oeuvre of stories. Often, Lao poems are written in what Koret (2000, 219) calls a "pattern of three" or "AAB pattern" in which a final monostich summarizes the preceding parallels. The AAB pattern is similarly fractal: it may be present within a single line, or within an entire story. Alternately, the final phrase may be purposely unvoiced, creating a monostich, as in the opening example about the naga and the river—my friend intended me to come to my own final conclusion. Her persistent silence triggered me to more closely examine her words. I was learning to hear the parallels, and to hear the silence that exists between parallels. Below is a simple AAB pattern poem improvised by a monk during a mine risk education training. I recorded a poetic transcription of his words, inductively drawing the poem out of my raw notes (Leavy 2009). I've added marks for the AAB pattern and included my own translation, maintaining the AAB form:

Baw dtaaii (A1)	Baw dtai (A2)
Dtaaii dtai (B)	
Don't die	Don't do it
We all die	

While the poem sounds dour in translation, it provoked laughter at the training session due to its gallows humor and clever repetition of only two sounds (with tonal and vowel-length variation). As he said it, the orating monk gestured to a poster of a farmer reaching down to pick up a cluster bomblet in his field—don't pick up the bomb! This short poem demonstrates another feature of parallelism: successful parallels often feed off a central tension or contradiction within the poem. The final line summarizes the tension: regardless of the risk reduction practices one learns, everyone is going to die in the end. The poem does not resolve this tension, only presents it as a fact of (Buddhist) existence.

Fieldwork in Socialist Asia

In my research practice, I engaged parallels as a quality of ethnographic research and hazardous data. While my broader claim is that this method of attention is applicable to hazardous field sites more generally, the present analysis is rooted in my experiences carrying out fieldwork in Laos. In this narrower sense, I am making a claim for the necessity of fieldwork methods for socialist Asia. By making this claim, I am first recognizing the difference between socialist Asia and postsocialist Russia and Eastern Europe. Like Sarah Turner (2013), in her pioneering account of fieldwork in upland socialist Asia, I read post-Soviet scholarship as its own field, not necessarily relevant to the study of modern Asian socialist states. The USSR and its communist satellites fell during the late 1980s. Liberalization and market integration occurred rapidly in communist regions, including Laos and its neighbors China and Vietnam. And yet while communism collapsed in some areas, Laos, China, and Vietnam instituted gradual economic reforms while remaining centralized and single-party states. Urban Vientiane, in particular, is at the forefront of Laos's fraught opening to Western developers and investors. Vientiane's resulting mix of Party elites, social elites, and Western developers is equal parts economic frontier and authoritarian capital city—police checkpoints at every major intersection, entire city blocks under redevelopment. This regional context presents fieldwork challenges, particularly to Westerners and ethnographers, that are distinct from those experienced in other areas of the world (and form a pattern that goes beyond the simple truth that all field sites are different). "Relationships in the field are a result of specific power structures," and the analysis of fieldwork dilemmas is a critical, but often underrepresented, way to study power (Turner 2013, 9). For example, ongoing policies of control over the movement of foreigners within Laos had a direct and immediate effect on my ability to access rural field sites. While recognizing the heterogeneity of my interlocutors' descriptions of Laos's socioeconomic system (socialist, postsocialist, late socialist, directed capitalist, centralized market economy, etc.), I choose to refer to Laos as socialist to reflect my experience conducting fieldwork in this region.

Almost no data on fieldwork in Laos exist, a lacuna that partially inspired Turner's volume. This absence is directly related to fieldworkers' experiences navigating the Party state. Pierre Petit (2013) interprets this lack of information on fieldwork in Laos as a form of self-protection in authoritarian contexts, especially against losing access already hard won from Lao gatekeepers. This has the unintended effect of reifying a leviathan state, unexamined and often assumed omnipresent in Lao society. Interactions with gatekeepers, normally sidelined as the prefieldwork negotiation, constitute valuable ethnographic data on the state itself. Considering these state-researcher interactions as a form of ethnography "sheds light on the very basic mechanisms of the state as experienced from within. Problematic situations such as refusals, bureaucratic harassment, no-reply strategies, denunciations and (self-)censorship paradoxically help to draw an 'outline' or 'contre-jour' portrait of the state" (Petit 2013, 144). Interactions were patterned by repetitious silences that the researcher might, paradoxically, identify via omission. Holly High noticed that, even told in intimate settings, stories of the state "carried the emotional charge of speaking that which must not be said but which, nonetheless, is said compulsively and repetitiously" (2014, 89). Such stories were, often intentionally, lacking links to actual persons or events (they could not be factually verified). There is no public, open discussion of the state in Laos. Instead, accounts that describe the "real" workings of the state are "a public secret . . . communicated to visitors in a way that shows this knowledge is supposed to be unknown, but that it is necessary to know nevertheless if one is to have any operational efficacy" (High 2014, 90). Ambiguous procedures and public secrets frustrate efforts to explain standard fieldwork practices— and also indicate the enculturation of paranoia in interactions with officials (and fieldworkers).

Conducting fieldwork in China, Mette H. Hansen argues for the impossibility of carrying out conventional ethnographic research in socialist Asia due to the power of Party gatekeepers. Hansen refers to this as "walking in the footsteps of the Communist Party" (2006, 82). I know this feeling. Due to travel restrictions on foreign researchers, it was far easier for me to study my NGO-worker interlocutors in Vientiane, the capital city, than to conduct fieldwork in rural communities. On one of the few occasions when I managed to officially travel with my NGO research hosts to a rural site, I was dismayed to discover that our van was being covertly escorted by two trucks full of soldiers "for our protection. Because if anything happened, the district would be responsible," a Lao interlocutor told me. My interlocutor politely resisted my queries for details on "anything" happening, which made her caution more sinister. Two trucks, one a few kilometers ahead and one a few kilometers behind. The soldiers were instructed to arrive in the village before us, alert the villagers to our visit, and leave before we arrived. It was evident that I was not supposed to know that we were being supervised. We were traveling to a remote area dominated by non-Lao, non-Buddhist communities, a region characterized by my colleagues as barely governable and extremely poor. In Lao ecopolitical cosmology, forested rural peripheries (and their inhabitants) are often thought to be uncivilized, lacking the internal capacity for social order (Singh 2012). The escort was silent and discreet—I never saw them or their guns—but their presence haunted my fieldwork. I found myself cultivating a what-if ethics: what if "anything happened"? How could I fully comprehend the risks to my subjects and myself when an open discussion of hazards was, itself, a hazard? On future trips, I pursued less official transportation.

These kinds of uncomfortable situations may be analyzed toward the study of fieldwork methods in socialist Asia and, doubly, toward the ethnography of authoritarian power in contemporary Laos. An expat interlocutor who similarly discovered his secret escort was deeply shaken; though a pacifist, he was unable to refuse his armed escort. Was the aid program he was scouting worth the risks implied by the soldiers? He refused the logic that linked the provision of services to armed surveillance, but found himself implicated in it nonetheless. In our interactions with the armed guards assigned to us, I and my NGO research hosts enacted a kind of distance. In the village, I was hyperconscious to not say or do anything that might cause the guards behind me to threaten the villagers. When an NGO interlocutor gave me the opportunity to interview local shamans about spirit cult practices, I declined their offer, privately pointing out to my interlocutor that such practices were sometimes suppressed by the state. I couldn't know how my interest would be interpreted by those invisible watchers. In adopting this attitude of cultivated distance, my scholarship became entangled in the everyday experience of authoritarian power.

"I Swear I'm Not a Spy"

I extend these concerns with the entanglement of authoritarianism and scholarship to the development of fieldwork methods in the region. Fieldwork in Laos is impacted by ongoing, insidious, and violent geopolitical processes: most relevant to my analysis of hazardous research, my fieldwork was riddled with paranoia about espionage and surveillance. Nearly every one of my interlocutors voiced concerns about spies, either that they were being spied on, or that I was a spy. A friend had warned me that "researcher equals spy" and that I should be careful about how I was introduced to officials—without my having to raise this concern, my NGO hosts introduced me as a student or an intern, never as a researcher. It became apparent to me during the first months of my research that I needed to critically address the pervasive paranoia of my interlocutors. I took up this challenge in two ways: first, to examine paranoia as ethnographic evidence, and second, as an incitement to methodological innovation.

Fieldwork in Southeast Asia is part of a covert history of anthropologists working as spies. The first American Anthropological Association Statement on Ethics was written in response to anthropologists working for the American government during the Vietnam-American War. During the war, some American missionaries, researchers, and aid workers were enrolled as covert culture experts—part of the reason that the current Lao regime is nervous about ethnographic research. I could trace this history further back, to Franz Boas's famous tirade against the American government hiring anthropologists as spies during World War I. He wrote that these anthropological spies "have done the greatest possible disservice to scientific inquiry. In consequence of their acts every nation will look with distrust upon the visiting foreign investigator who wants to do honest work, suspecting sinister designs" (Boas 1919). At the time, Boas was censured by the American Anthropological Association for his critiques. The council that met to censure Boas was later determined to have been infiltrated by the very spies that Boas decried.

Today, in contemporary Laos, this is a history that I inhabit. At one of my first interviews, the chief's council of the village convened to determine if I was a risk to their community. The chief's council brought a copy of my Study Information Letter (which was then my consent document) heavily highlighted in neon yellow. The council sat in a semicircle behind me, covertly observing me as I began to go over the consent document with my interlocutor. I prolonged going over the document until, it seemed, they gave him a silent sign of support. There was a noticeable loosening of tension, and my interlocutor began to smile. At this point, the council rose as a group, leaving me to continue the interview on my own. I do not know how they decided that I was not a spy—it seemed inappropriate to turn to face them and ask. At the same time, I assumed that my interlocutor was using the legitimacy of the chief's council to hide his own illegal war scrap trade and stockpiling of live ordnance—which he detailed to me only after the council had left.

This early interview was my first lesson in how to navigate the subtleties of subject protections in Laos. Just beyond the small house where we conducted the interview, soldiers with AK-47s patrolled the street and enforced a strict curfew for foreigners. The home had only three walls such that I could hear the distinct sound of military boots passing behind me at regular intervals. There had recently been rebel activity in the area, and the local constabulary were closely monitoring foreigners, ostensibly for our protection. In the absence of public debate, risk proliferates in partial connections—for example, via an implied connection between an American researcher and rebel groups in the jungle supposedly funded by Americans. Hazard might mean increased suspicion from the local constabulary, or, more severely, my interlocutor being accused of supplying rebels with bombs from his secret stockpile. The exact consequences of speaking overtly were often unclear and rarely voiced; people recognized hazards without having to know what they were. The institutions and individuals that determine what information is hazardous were not held responsible for making their actions transparent. Rather, the opaque qualities of suppression or reprisal perpetuated the state's control over knowledge. Ultimately, this early encounter prompted me to amend my research protocols to make the written consent document optional. I had learned that my Study Information Letter could be used as evidence for or against myself and my interlocutors. In that town, at that time, meeting privately with an American was hazardous.

References to spies punctuated my interviews. If we met in a public spot, interlocutors would often point out who in the area they thought was tailing them. Such comments could be presented in a playful way—or could carry a real charge of danger. In one memorable interview at a café, I met with a religious leader who had previously told me about his colleagues being threatened by soldiers, shot point blank in front of him, or simply disappeared. When a wealthy, large Lao man with a military demeanor, but dressed in plain clothes, entered the empty café and sat at a nearby table, my interlocutor locked eyes with me fiercely. Without breaking eye contact, he pitched his voice louder and said, "I don't hide from [the] government." After that, every word he said was voiced to carry to that other listener—the state. Our interview acquired the quality of being parallel; another version of that interview existed for the acknowledged, but silent, listener at the table next to us. Being told that an interlocutor's colleague was recently shot by the police for collaborating with foreign groups, and being spied on during interviews with this interlocutor, pushes me to reassess my own, and my interlocutor's, protection practices. Our parallel interview (with me and with the spy) heightened my attention to what could be said and what could only be said by not speaking directly ("I don't hide from [the] government"). While my concerns about omissions in data differed greatly from interlocutors' concerns about being disappeared by the police, our sensibilities aligned within the domain of subject-researcher protections. In this domain, my growing familiarity with parallelism was an important tool for recognizing and communicating hazards in research—especially in situations where the discussion of risk was a hazard in and of itself. In fieldwork, interviews such as these imply that the parallel of silence is listening (the parallel of silence is not speaking).* Listening for the unsaid requires a kind of paranoia from the interviewer, an attentive ear that is tuned to the fears of those being interviewed.

My interlocutors' fears of espionage had other unexpected consequences. After I spent a week conducting fieldwork with a bomb clearance operator, the team leader confided in me that she had agreed to my fieldwork request partially assuming that I was an American spy sent to check up on her team's use of funds and proper handling of explosives. Working under this assumption, she felt that she could not refuse my research request without "giving up the game." In private conversation, I told her, forcefully, "I swear I am not a spy." Ethnographic encounters such as this one highlight the contingency of research ethics. I could not have known that this culture of paranoia would facilitate my access to this field site prior to entering the site. The team leader's confession of paranoia, ironically, indexed her increasing comfort with my research presence. Ethnographic examples such as this make

---

* I note the possible connections to Eve Kosofsky Sedgwick's (2002) paranoid inquiry. Suspicion and paranoia prompt the researcher to uncover systems of oppression as a means of knowledge production in the social sciences.

plain the total paranoia in place. Having been variously suspected of spying, and suspecting others of spying, the arbitrariness of the paranoia is obvious. These fears of espionage have a fantastical quality, while also betraying an element of parody—almost amateurish, what Begona Aretxaga (2000, 60) describes as "bar terrorism," like tall tales told over drinks at a bar, in which "state terrorism [reveals] the state more as a parody" of its own claims to total power. In this highly charged political context, the reality of espionage is almost beside the point. The feeling exists quite apart from the actual capacity of the Lao state to carry out complex surveillance, which is generally held to be very low.

Fingers-Crossed Ethnography

Three days before I left Laos, my research assistant revealed that he had been lying to cover up our research together. Every time he accompanied me on interviews or site visits, he told his colleagues and employer that he was "going to the Ministry of Finance to sign paperwork." It was the perfect alibi, since the ministry was known for its arbitrary paperwork and interminable waiting time. He used the government's own inefficiencies to hide his activities from the government. I was surprised and troubled by his secrecy, since he had previously told me that he saw our work as contributing to his professional goals. But his refusal to interact with the government was marked: the few times that I asked him to accompany me on government visits, he perpetually deferred the meeting such that we never attended together. He would advise me not to go. Over the course of our work together, my impression was that he was trying to protect himself from government suspicion (for working with a foreign researcher) and also trying to protect me from suspicion (for being a foreign researcher). Simultaneously, but without our having openly discussed it, I returned his courtesy by never revealing his identity to my government interlocutors.

My own and my assistant's mutual secrecy highlights the contingency of subject and researcher protections. The two of us formed a relationship of parallel secrecy. Scholarship on fieldwork methods tends to compartmentalize methods from ethics, and researcher from subject protections. None of my methods manuals include a section on subject/researcher protections, though the topic of subject protections is briefly treated in some of them (Bernard 2011; Maxwell 1996). Even my manual for research on the violation of human rights does not include guidance on how to protect subjects or researchers inhabiting contexts of human-rights abuse (Reed and Pad-skocimaite 2012). The risks of fieldwork to the researcher are, surprisingly, rarely explored in methods manuals. Against this trend, some scholarship has examined the centrality of risks in fieldwork (Davies and Spencer 2010; Lee-Treweek and Linkogle 1999; Nordstrom and Robben 1996). These contemporary scholars are "making danger visible and explaining its relationship to data collection and the understanding of social phenomena" (Lee-Treweek and Linkogle 1999, 1). Intense experiences, notably feelings of surveillance, fundamentally altered my experience of being a fieldworker and the conditions of possibility for my research. Situating myself in this field site required me to cultivate my own paranoia. Warned by a colleague about a spy in the office, I was unsurprised when my desk was searched. I had, in preparation, stacked my desk with inane pamphlets. My field notes did not contain basic subject identifiers (subjects were assigned codes in the field); I never left field notes or transcripts at my desk. My colleagues' warnings rarely coalesced into overt fear; it was more like a repeated insistence on careful possibility.

This socially reinforced paranoia invites analysis of alternatives to the conventional ethics and method framework of ethnography. David Calvey (2008) critiques the modern anthropological fetish on ethics. Referencing my earlier discussion of anthropological espionage, Calvey explores the ethical use of covert research methods: pretending to be someone you're not in order to gather data in hazardous field sites. And while I do not employ covert research methods, I do respect the debate that Calvey is working to sustain in anthropology. This is a debate about what ethics looks like in practice, a reminder to make conscious decisions to address the hazards of knowledge production—to cultivate "situated ethics" (Calvey 2008, 906). He writes, "Engagement with the ethics of research is not a ritualistic tick box process that once done at the beginning of a project can then be obviated, but runs throughout the lifetime of a project" (2008, 909). My situated ethics required careful listening: at the end of an interview, as I was asking if there was anything an interlocutor wanted me to redact from my notes, she laughed and remarked, "No, the government of Laos already knows everything!" Her very phrase implied that she thought she was subject to government surveillance. I made the decision to anonymize and change some details of her story. I took these extra protections above those requested in part to protect her, and in part to protect myself. As other scholars have pointed out, "blinding" data may support results or detract from them

(Ponesse 2014). I find it fruitful, like Ponesse, to think of anonymity as a so-cial phenomenon that points to the wider contexts that make certain kinds of knowledge unsafe. Listening for speech by omission, my subject protec-tions should link to the real and silently implied hazards my informants risk by speaking with me.

In dangerous contexts, Calvey often felt himself to be doing "a type of 'fin-gers crossed ethnography' where [his] luck might have run out" (2008, 913). I cannot pinpoint the difference between feeling safe and feeling unsafe in a field site. Coming home early, I once encountered two unknown men repair-ing the ceiling lights; after they left, I noticed what looked like little surveil-lance holes in the ceiling of my apartment. Cleaning my desk of sensitive documents as a precaution against searches began to feel routine. My field notes filled up with what-ifs. Here's one: A young, well-dressed Lao woman followed my husband and me as we strolled through downtown Vientiane looking for a café in which to sit and enjoy tea together. The woman followed us into a small café, choosing a table near us. She approached our table and offered us red rambuton fruit from a bag. We declined. She left the café, then came back shortly without the bag of fruit, ordered a coffee, and sat at a table next to us. A few minutes later, she approached us and said, without any preamble, "May I ask you some questions about Lao politics?" I declined with a smile, thinking that no one talks about politics in public in Laos. My husband answered, gamely, but only with descriptions of Philippine politics (he grew up in Manila). Repeatedly she attempted to get him to say that Lao officials were corrupt. Realizing he would not say it, she left just as abruptly as she arrived. The encounter struck me as an overly blunt instance of spy reconnaissance. In encounters such as this, I crossed my fingers and nothing happened—but what if? What if my assistant's boss had found out he was working with a foreign researcher? What if the woman at the café was a spy? What if I had answered the woman's questions? What if my husband had not been coy enough to restrict his talk to the Philippines? Fieldwork ethics are always uncertain, partial, and necessarily contingent on the knowledge and skills acquired in the field.

Poems and Fieldpoems

I did not intend to write poems as part of my fieldwork practice. I found my-self compelled to do so once I was in the field and, as my Lao skills increased, slowly became aware of the unexpected parallel between my turn to poetry and my interlocutors' own practices. Other fieldworkers might not have felt compelled to write poems. My compulsion is not universal, but it does convey information about my fieldwork experience and the complexities of this field site. "Our slow integration into the field . . . by either loosening existing ties or forcing new adaptations, commonly generates new states and ways of being significant to the work we undertake" (Davies 2010, 47). In the present chapter, I chart my conceptual attunement to poetic parallelism (learning to "think in two ways") and its implications for conducting hazardous research.*

Let me describe the first instance of my poetic compulsion: In the early months of 2012, I traveled with a bomb clearance operator to the Plain of Jars in Xieng Khouang Province. This was my first trip outside the insular capital of Vientiane. When I arrived in Phonsavan, the provincial capital, I was immediately struck with a puzzling vertigo. It took me several days to figure out that this feeling was caused by my perception of the eerie flatness of the area, its lingering war contamination, plus the present construction boom: a sense of things missing, coupled with a premonition of future construction and destruction. The Plain of Jars, and all its towns and villages, were completely destroyed by a decade of continuous bombings during the Vietnam-American War. The province was literally flattened, and then its towns rebuilt in bits and pieces, often using war scrap as building material (see figure 1.2). The epitome of Phonsavan urban development was the dual-model bomb clearance and construction company, and several shops of this type could be found in the town center. The ground beneath Phonsavan was not systematically cleared prior to its founding, meaning that clearance is ongoing and haphazard. People live with the possibility of total destruction: a café owner exclaimed to me, "There is a five-hundred-pound bomb under this café, too big to remove, so we built the cafe on top of it. . . . If there is an earthquake, the whole block is going to go *boom!*" Hulks of old artillery guns and other war paraphernalia strangely littered the new capital and its surrounds, slowly picked over by scavengers, or preserved by local officials as half-dismantled relics of the war. The ordnance in figure 1.3 was displayed in the yard of a Phonsavan government office, loosely piled

* In future work, I will discuss the implications of poetry for ethnographic research— what I term fieldpoems—and how fieldpoetry might contribute to new forms of ethnographic research and argumentation.

FIGURE 1.2 Dismantled general-purpose bombs used as supports for a stilt house near Phonsavan, Xieng Khouang Province. Photo by the author.

FIGURE 1.3 Live explosive ordnance on display at a government office in Phonsavan, Xieng Khouang Province. Photo by the author.

by type—in this photo, a pile of cluster submunitions. Bombs were prominently featured in local architecture—often without first having been certified inert, as an interlocutor of mine discovered when he investigated the bombs that decorated his office. I could not convey this feeling accurately in my field notes or photographs, nor can I now in this passage.

I found myself writing my first poems in the field in order to record this experience:

FIELDPOEMS 1 AND 2

The Plain is the ash
sifted to everywhere
an expanse of itself

Flatness becomes
the houses, the craters
filled in by debris

Without occluding your own readings of this poem, let me say: here I am thinking through the ghostly flatness of Phonsavan after a decade of intense bombings. A bomb technician had described the bombing as "inefficient," meaning that many of the bombs deployed exploded upward (rather than outward), producing vast clouds of debris relative to the destruction. There was a literal sifting of soil. This flatness, in turn, enabled development built on craters, built with debris. Locals described filling in craters with the debris of houses in order to build good foundations for their houses. Dismantled bombs sometimes served as the supports for stilt houses "because the metal doesn't rot in the mud," my guide explained (see figure 1.2). As a research exercise, I later rewrote my first fieldpoem in a Lao style:

The Plain	The ash
sifted to everywhere	an expanse of itself
Flatness becomes	the craters
the houses	filled in by debris

Written in this style, the parallels that I was intuitively constructing become clearer. The columns may be read across or down for different resonances. The alternating flatness of the destroyed houses and the filled-in craters comes through with more strength. The visual parallel between the flat plain and the sifted, settling ash of the bombing is also much stronger. This poem was a crucial part of my recognizing this cycle of destruction/construction in postwar Laos.

Crafting these fieldpoems via ethnographic parallelism, I am drawing on a regional poetic tradition to develop my own distinct conceptual project. This poetic tradition, in turn, could be traced to regional cosmologies of pairs (not binary pairs like "up and down," but parallel pairs like "a pair of shoes"), which I attend to throughout the book (Errington 1990; Holt 2009). Parallels may be very similar (as a left shoe is similar to a right shoe) and yet never resolve into a single entity. A left and a right shoe together form a pair via their intra-action, their internal relations with each other. Parallels are not binaries or necessary opposites; nor do parallels necessarily equate one with the other or exchange one for the other. Rather, parallels have a relation to each other across a necessary gap, as two lines are parallel when they do not cross. They exist side by side. There is no requirement of dialectic resolution in which one dissolves into another, or in which the two merge into some higher or lower entity.

My approach draws on a rich tradition in anthropology and related social theories of holding specific field data and general theory in simultaneous tension (see, especially, Geertz 1973; Strathern 2004; Žižek 2009). My use of parallelism follows a tradition of writerly exploration in anthropology, a tradition that is fed by the fieldworker's own awareness of the complementarity between ethnographic data and theory. This mode of simultaneous attention is, for many fieldworkers, latent in their practice of ethnography: famously, Clifford Geertz's use of interpretive analysis includes a process of "continuous dialectical tacking between the most local of local detail and the most global of global structure in such a way as to bring them into simultaneous view" (1983, 69). Anthropological knowledge production already exists in parallel with the fields we study. Bill Maurer cultivates "lateral reasoning" as a response to his experiences negotiating the relations between data and theory: "Anthropology lies alongside the worlds of those I studied, not adjudicating theory and practice but transacting the parallel knowledges, the paralanguages . . . between subjects and objects of inquiry, and their lateralizations, their interconnections with each other, and with 'me,' 'anthropology,' and 'critique'" (2005, xv). These various forms of "para-work" constitute a type of reasoning that exists alongside the experiences of the fieldworker and of those she is studying. There is no necessary congruity between theory and experience; rather, the relation of one to the other is that of parallelism, generative tension, perhaps even necessary contradiction. The paradoxes are data, too. This mode of inquiry invites comparison without commensurability, and without recourse to a more fundamental background or baseline that grounds critique itself. As a writer, I activate this parallel process in my writing such that the tensions experienced in the field are referenced in my theorizing of field data.

These concerns with data and theory are also examined in the anthropological study of war and violence, a topic that I return to in chapter 3. There again, I employ the concept of parallelism to negotiate the gap between theories and experiences of violence. I employ a brief example from Pat Frank's pioneering apocalyptic novel, *Alas, Babylon*, to introduce my analytic point. Frank, in his introduction to the novel, juxtaposes the word "bomb" with the experience of feeling an explosion: "A man who has been shaken by a two-ton blockbuster [bomb] has a frame of reference. He can equate the impact of an H-bomb with his own experience, even though the H-bomb blast is a million times more powerful than the shock he endured. To someone who has never felt a bomb, bomb is only a word" (2013, vi). Frank explains his quandary in terms of bodily feeling; these are words wrested from experience. How might our concept and theory frames embrace this absence of a shared "frame of reference" for experience? It is not that the word "bomb" is wrong, or that only veterans of war zones can understand war literature and scholarship. Rather, the apparatus of equating words and feelings is itself brought into doubt. Approached in this manner, the gap between the word "bomb" and the feeling of a bomb exploding is part of the data, itself, that requires wrestling and struggle on the part of the writer and her audience. This kind of writing challenges the assumption that theories are adequate to reality, or that reading theory should be a passive experience of equating words with experience. My goal, instead, is to craft modes of writing and theorizing that attend to the parallel experiences of research subjects, scholarly peers, and other members of our communities. Poetry is one way that I activate these parallels between experience and theory.

Parallelism plays around with different kinds of knowledge. Data on the Secret War are often contradictory or unavailable—and poetry is a generous kind of knowledge, open to multiple interpretations. Rather than trying to wrangle with multiple, suspect information on the war, the poem gives up the search for single answers and embraces ambiguity. My fieldpoems are accurate without being intelligible in a conventional, narrative way. As ethnographic data, these poems work precisely because poetry resists the quick equivalence of experience and knowledge. Sandra L. Faulkner advocates for the use of poetry in research as a means of preserving wonder in data: "[Poetry] resists itself; the fact that poetry resists itself means we can experience wonder, rediscover pleasure in our inability to make the word intelligible" (2009, 16). Poetry's capacity to resist knowledge preserves crucial qualities of ambiguity and uncertainty present in my data.

FIELDPOEM 17

A bomb is under this café
500 pounds, too big to remove
I sip my mulberry tea

This poem developed out of my interaction with the Phonsavan café owner referenced at the beginning of this section. Compared with my earlier prose description, this poem does a better job of conveying my sense of surreality, a normalcy punctured by latent danger. It accomplishes this, in part, by eschewing lengthy description and juxtaposing two carefully chosen details: mulberry tea and a five-hundred-pound bomb. I winnowed my experience of hazard down to this taut pair. Writing under conditions of hazard, this winnowing process may be somewhat analogous to scrubbing data for purposes of subject protection. During the writing of this chapter, the field notes of my encounter at this café went through a process of anonymization whereby details were changed to protect my interlocutor's identity; in contrast, this fieldpoem did not go through a separate anonymization process because an analogous wrestling with identity, silence, and disclosure was embedded in my writing of the poem in the field. There are no subject identifiers in this poem, and almost no subject identifiers in any of my fieldpoems.

Let me elaborate my point with a few, carefully curated ethnographic details: this poem is a place marker for the café owner's illegal expertise in bomb clearance, euphemistically known in the clearance sector as village clearance volunteering. The café owner cleared bombs found in the routine construction of Phonsavan. The five-hundred-pound bomb she found during the construction of her own café, however, was too big for her to remove. The irony (that the bomb was underneath the café of a village clearance volunteer) did not escape her. Unspoken in our conversation was our shared knowledge that her clearance activities were doubly illegal: it is illegal to conduct unofficial clearance; and it is illegal for a civilian to possess bombs. Like blank space on the page, the poem is structured by unspoken possibilities: being charged with possessing a bomb that dropped forty years ago, now buried under the café; being killed by a bomb while sipping tea in peacetime. The brevity of the poem was, itself, inspired by the absence of any direct references to these oblique risks and illegalities—all things that were common knowledge and yet usually discussed only indirectly. And so the poem speaks indirectly, too. As Audra Simpson describes in her own wrestling with "ethnographic refusal," these moments of nondisclosure imply "an ethnographic calculus of what you need to know and what I refuse to write . . . for the express purpose of protecting the concerns of the community" (2014, 105). Leaving gaps in an ethnographic account acknowledges the power systems that pertain in field research, informing relations between researcher and interlocutor. "Those of us writing about [issues that go unspoken] can also 'refuse'" to speak (Simpson 2014, 11). With this kind of oblique data, I strive for faithful descriptions where factual ones are risky or impossible. I am increasingly convinced that an accurate ethnography of Laos will also be oblique, riven by silences—a ghostly, read-between-the-lines, fingers-crossed kind of ethnography.

Conclusion: Hazardous Research Methods

Parallelism is an immensely rich and creative practice. In the domain of ethnographic method, parallelism implies an ethics of attention to contradictions, multiplicities, and silences. In this chapter, I have used parallelism as a conceptual frame for understanding hazards in fieldwork: not only as a means of communicating hazards in the field but also as a means of recording and analyzing hazards as data. Simultaneously, my use of poetry in the field was largely a response to feelings of hazard. Lao parallelism stimulated me to contemplate the deeper significance of my intuitive impulse to field-poetry. As I have made clear, parallelism does not necessarily take the form of poetry; nor do fieldpoems necessarily take the form of parallel hemistichs. More accurately, the hazards of this field site inspired me to develop a new ethnographic sensibility, one crafted via poems and parallels. Expanding my initial claim to developing methods for fieldwork in socialist Asia, it is my hope that this method may have more general significance wherever ethnographers encounter hazards in fieldwork.

Like the researcher-poet Faulkner, I ask of a fieldpoem: "Why is there a reason for speech rather than silence?" (Faulkner 2009, 92). Repeatedly presented with this question in the course of studying postwar Laos, I found myself reading war poetry. There is a long and full tradition of poets choosing to address war, violence, and social justice issues with poems. Mahmoud Darwish's poem on the 1982 bombing of Beirut foregrounds being bombed with descriptions of mundane acts, like fetching the newspaper: "What am I searching for? I open the door several times, but find no newspaper. Why am I looking for the paper when buildings are falling in all directions? Is that not writing enough?" (1995, 23). The bombs themselves are words, and the words bombs that explode on the page. This powerfully imaginative move aligns the reader's experience of reading with the poet's experience of being bombed. Darwish collapses the distance between being and knowing, thereby, almost magically, working against the difficulty of describing his destroyed neighborhood. Taking this insight back to ethnography, I understand fieldpoems as a process of "poetic inquiry . . . to synthesize experience in a direct and affective way" (Prendergast 2009, xxii), thereby tightening the connections between knowledge and experience and making that knowledge more accessible to audiences with diverse experiences. The poet's focus on the details of the everyday at war disrupts assumptions about "everyday" and "war." When aligned with ethnography, such poems root new theories in the intimacy, affectivity, and experience of hazards. Poetry helps me to think through a monk saying "We all die" even while educating people on safer farming methods for war-contaminated fields. There is an existential particularity in (post)war zones that is deeply responsive to ethnographic and poetic attention.

The persistent danger of military waste in my field site is the always-present background to my theorizing of hazards. There is a poetic parallel between hazardous data and dangerous military waste. I use the word "hazard" in contradistinction to the overdetermining vocabulary of "danger" and "risk" common in the explosives clearance sector. "Hazard" is a broader conceptual frame that enables me to trace parallels between, for example, the terror of state violence and the risk of a bomb exploding. My analysis of hazardous data overlaps, but does not fully eclipse, the analysis of danger in military waste zones. And yet, in my thinking and writing, I continually circle back to the dangers of explosive military waste. Subterranean explosives, lying latent in the earth fifty years after the Vietnam-American War began, are a counterpoint to my experience of espionage, surveillance, and government violence. In some of my poems, unexploded bombs serve as metonyms for the threat of political violence. These are threats that I could not fully remove from fieldwork. The monks' risk education poem embraces the always incomplete task of removing risks and reducing suffering: proper risk education does not prevent a cluster bomblet from exploding when triggered. Societies and cultures are complex; hazards, rather than being fieldwork obstacles that must necessarily be removed, are a form of cultural complexity important in ethnographic research.

Rilke opined that each poem is the outcome of "having-been-in-danger" (quoted in Hirshfield 2015, 42): having been at extremity, having suffered, or having been injured. My fieldpoems were often responses to my own or my interlocutors' experiences at extremity. Yet it can be difficult to identify when one has entered an extreme in a field site marked by paranoia; where a placid field may hide land mines beneath. My paranoia demonstrated aspects of contemporary Lao culture, while also raising methodological and ethical issues about hazardous fieldwork. This recursive relation between writing and fieldwork is not restricted to poetry, though my experience was that hazardous fieldwork compelled a poetic sensibility attuned to Lao parallelism. In this final poem, I list obvious sources of hazard (artillery guns, military bunkers). Yet the guns were rusting, long unused, and the bunkers were greening and locked. They failed to explain my growing sense of unease and were more like evidence of my own misdirection. Military wastes, despite their abject danger, were not the hazards that required my attention; police harassment and government surveillance were much greater hazards in fieldwork. In the final line of the poem, the parallel form conveys my ambivalent feelings about entering this field site. I am landing, an American, on an airstrip built during the Vietnam-American War to accommodate bombing raids in the region. The poem takes the classic account of the anthropologist entering the field and makes it sinister. Written with the benefit of hindsight, the poem captures my premonition of the hazards of research:

FIELDPOEM 31
Entrances and Exits

I step down from the plane
I am rushing towards something, something unpleasant
Past artillery guns rusting by the runway
and the green slopes of earthwork bunkers
every hill has a door

abandoned   entrances and exits

"The Rice Is More Delicious after Bomb Clearance"

dig this rice field with a shovel
so the rice will be more delicious—
each two white grains
precious as two eyes

2 • GHOST MINE

———

It is an optical illusion to attribute these mutilations to accidents. Actually,
accidents are the result of mutilations that took place long ago in the embryo of
our world. . . . The loss occurred long before it was visibly taken into account.
—ERNST JÜNGER, *The Glass Bees* (1957)

Battlefields into Marketplaces

In the first few years of the Renovation, as Laos opened its borders to Western liberal intervention, private investors from over thirty countries initi-
ated projects in mining, forestry, and other natural resource industries in
Laos (Phraxayavong 2009, 164). With the rising and falling of social science
research as a practice of imperial attention, this period saw a burgeoning of
scholarly interest in Laos, a field of study that had largely lain fallow after
the war (see especially Evans 1998; Goscha and Ivarson 2003; Gun 1998;
Pholsena 2006). The early Renovation period also included Laos's first official explosives clearance programs, carried out by both humanitarian and
private operators. Private explosives clearance operators rushed to meet the
needs of industrialists capitalizing on Laos's unextracted, but heavily war-
contaminated, natural resources. This natural wealth was itself a product of

war, secured from exploitation by three decades of continuous conflict, the American embargo, and the lack of local expertise or infrastructure. These resources were accessed, first, via clearance programs that prepared safe areas for industrial activities. Explosives clearance and economic opportunity are grounded in the same contaminated soils.

Out of this dynamic of danger/opportunity arose the war ghost, returning unbidden and unknown despite the suppression of any sustained public discussion of postwar violence. The war ghost was a social figure central to people's experiences of ongoing violence, particularly with regard to how people related to military waste. In this chapter, I examine the haunting of Sepon, a new industrial center in Savannakhet Province. The small town of Sepon was located in a remote, sparsely populated area along the mountainous border between Laos and Vietnam. Laos lies along the spine of the Annamite and related mountain ranges. Most of the country is sparsely populated highland, mountainous jungle; most of the country is the periphery of the lowland cities. These rural, seemingly marginal areas have become important targets of Renovation reforms, while also being among the poorest, most remote, most ethnically diverse, and most war-contaminated parts of the country. The Sepon borderland was once part of the Ho Chi Minh Trail, the infamous supply line to North Vietnam during the Vietnam-American War. The trail was heavily bombed during the war and remains massively contaminated with bombs to this day. Digging into the middle of this contaminated landscape, the Minerals and Metals Group (MMG) Lane Xang Metals Limited mine in Sepon (hereafter, the Lane Xang gold mine), a focus in this chapter, was simultaneously a source of great wealth and extreme danger. Workers at this remote mine were digging up more than mere metal: the gold mine was contaminated by live ordnance, rich in archaeological artifacts, and haunted by ancient spirits and the hungry ghosts of war victims. The gold mine was also a ghost mine, a place where one digs up ghosts or perhaps becomes a ghost oneself.*

Thinking through what remains, in this chapter I develop a hauntology of military waste. My thinking on this topic is indebted to Jacques Derri-

---

* I draw the term "ghost mine" from my ethnographic data on haunting in Sepon. I want to make clear that my use of this term is distinct from the sometimes colloquial use of "ghost" to refer to corruption in the development sector (e.g., a corrupt project is a "ghost project"). At no point in my research in Sepon did I hear stories or encounter evidence of corruption at the mine.

da's hauntology and the scholarship it has inspired ([1993] 2006; see, for example, Derrida et al. 1999; Gordon 2008). In his original formulation, Derrida evokes haunting in the English sense of the term: the presence of frightening ghosts, or an obsession or fixation on a troubling memory. Haunting indicates an unexpected relation, or recursion, between the past and the present, or between two things that are supposedly incompatible. I respond to these scholarly provocations in line with Byron J. Good's (2015, 68) call to create an ethnographic hauntology that takes ghosts seriously as social actors and haunting as a social process. To craft a locally specific hauntology, I draw on more recent scholarship on war ghosts and war waste in contemporary Laos, Vietnam, and Cambodia (see especially Gustafsson 2009; Kwon 2008; Tappe and Pholsena 2013). By choosing to engage with literature on religion, ghosts, and spirits, I am activating sensibilities that often lie latent in the scholarship on postwar Southeast Asia. Each item of ordnance, each crater or grave, contributes to "a sense of a landscape as imbued with malevolent agency" (Tappe and Pholsena 2013, 7). Elaine Russell remarks that war waste contamination in Laos "haunts and shapes the everyday lives of the rural population" (2013, 96). What is the relation between an ethnographer's sense of "malevolent agency" and her interlocutors' experiences of being haunted? The present chapter continues my examination of perception in ethnographic fieldwork, here articulated as an attention to traces, remains, and ghosts that appear in the ethnographic record. How can we theorize this malevolence, or haunting, particularly in relation to overt signs of prosperity, such as rapid development and economic growth? Four decades after the war ended, unexploded ordnance is being dug up, literally still alive. The gold mine/ghost mine parallel brings to the fore the ambiguity of the present revival as, simultaneously, a resurrection of things buried. My discussion of parallelism in the previous chapter enables my present argument for simultaneous revival/ruination at the Lane Xang mine. In this way, I aim to argue from the parallel or, more precisely, from the resonant gap between seemingly contradictory parallels, to argue from the position of the ghost neither dead nor alive (or from that of the live bomb, buried alive).

In the flush of new regional opportunities following the collapse of the Soviet Union, Thai prime minister Chatichai Choonhavan called for all of Indochina to transform "from a battlefield to a marketplace" (quoted in Phraxayavong 2009, 163–64). In Laos, the transformation of battlefields into marketplaces occurred through a mix of Western NGOs and international financial institutions, as well as significant investments from over thirty countries (Phraxayavong 2009). Prime Minister Chatichai's famous call for postwar transformation belies the persisting presence of explosive military waste in the soil and water beneath the new shopping malls, industrial mines, office complexes, and roads. I examine Sepon as a target for this kind of ambivalent postwar transformation. The study of the haunting of Sepon contributes to my larger analysis of the transition from battlefields to liberal nation-states, integrated into the global market, and the reconstruction and rehabilitation practices that attend these transformations. The Lane Xang gold mine is Laos's first and largest mining operation, and the first major economic project under the Renovation reforms (the state partly owns the mine). How are the remains of war addressed in these processes of revival, and with what consequences for those who live in war-impacted areas? In Sepon, a massively contaminated former battlefield has been transformed into a literal gold mine for the Party state—and meanwhile, ghosts ambiguously manifest, challenging the state's ability to fully transform battlefields into marketplaces. The bombs, and the ghosts, remain.

Savannakhet, whose name means City of Paradise, is a mountainous rural province in southern Laos characterized by religious and ethnic diversity (and disproportionate poverty). Sharing opposite borders with Thailand and Vietnam, the province has historically functioned as a transit and trading center between the three countries. It is a core Party stronghold (one of the earliest liberated zones), the most war-contaminated province in the country, and the current target of major economic reform. The extravagant wealth of the Lane Xang gold mine and other local industries, concentrated in the hands of Party leaders and others, has brought with it major temple renovations and palaces in the area. Sepon also hosts the local headquarters of several foreign organizations, including an American MIA/POW mission and several bomb clearance operations. Despite its tiny size, the town of Sepon boasts connections to people in the highest offices of the Lao state, major international corporations, governments, and NGOs. In this chapter, I examine ambivalent experiences of development via a prominent Sepon temple renovation and a series of spirit possessions at the nearby Lane Xang gold mine. A study of Sepon brings to the fore the haunting of Laos's revival. Postwar development, authoritarian rule, and religious revival converge in this City of Paradise.

Old and New Sepon

In order to understand these processes of revival in the ruins, I begin by introducing the two parallel urban centers of Sepon: the old French provincial capital and, six kilometers distant, the new socialist town. Old Sepon, the former French capital, was completely destroyed by air bombardment during the war. In recent years, people have begun moving back into the ruins; the town, at present, is a small clutter of wooden stilt houses bordered by a river on three sides. The houses are spaced by the huge craters of air drop bombs and the regular foundation stones of the ruined brick buildings of the original French capital. Stone foundation blocks or stairways, leading into empty air, are oriented along streets that are invisible under the carpet of underbrush. The demarcation between the town and the surrounding forest is porous—trees grow everywhere. In the former town square, cows nose through slopes of brick debris for tender shoots. Perched atop one of these piles is a large walk-in vault, the remains of the French bank, now overgrown with a half century of moss and mold. This small, squat room was the only structure to remain standing in Sepon after ten years of nearly constant bombardment. Not far from the vault is a newly built school and the reconstructed village temple, Wat Sepon Gao (Old Sepon Temple), the only prewar building in Sepon that has ever been rebuilt. On the temple exterior, the remaining original wall is pockmarked with the percussion of shrapnel, the holes left intentionally fresh (see figure 2.1).

Up until fairly recently, the ruins of Old Sepon were abandoned. After the former French capital was destroyed, the new regime selected a location to be the new Sepon. For ease of reading and analysis, I use the term "new" to mark the more recent Sepon in distinction to the colonial ruins, though it is common practice to refer to the region as Sepon and, within that region, the two towns as Sepon and Old Sepon. I defer to the more general term (Sepon) when I am discussing the larger region inclusive of both urban centers. New Sepon, built along socialist plans, exists in parallel with the ruins of Old Sepon, only a few kilometers away. Old Sepon has bomb craters, piles of debris, cow pastures, and a half-ruined Buddhist temple; New Sepon has running water, electricity, a multistory hotel, local headquarters for several mining or other industrial operations, truck repair shops, and a market. New Sepon was to be a very different kind of city, built with a straight, paved road connecting it to the new regime's provincial capital. As the only developed town in these rural highlands, it is a magnet for industrial activity in

FIGURE 2.1 The original, remaining wall of Wat Sepon Gao, decorated
with streamers for the fund-raiser. Photo by the author.

the region. The town is not centered around a Buddhist temple, but instead
holds at its heart a collection of government offices and a dissolute, graying
monument to the revolution. It is a very tiny town, and it takes me less than
fifteen minutes to walk from one end to another along the single paved road,
Route 9.

In a not-too-distant era, this part of Route 9 was known as the "death
road," an especially dangerous and strategic area of the Ho Chi Minh Trail
(Pholsena 2013). During the war, Route 9 was scattered with land mines,
bombs, craters, and the dead; today, the road is paved and well maintained,
and almost all physical remains of the war along the road proper have been
cleared (see figure 2.2). The road's contemporary revival, as an economic
corridor through Sepon, is fraught: "Sepon villagers are no longer con-
fronted with a landscape in ruins on Route 9. . . . To villagers in this impoverished rural area, the two-lane paved road both constitutes and represents
economic development, but is also a place of darker times, of memories of
violence and rift" (Pholsena 2013, 158). For me, as an ethnographer traveling on Route 9 to conduct fieldwork, the road acted as a kind of unexpected
path to a ghostly domain to which I didn't necessarily know I was traveling.

FIGURE 2.2 New Sepon was an industrial town built along the
paved Route 9. Photo by the author.

As Achille Mbembe describes of travelers in the postcolonial ruins of Cam-
eroon, the road "open[s], unbeknownst to us, onto the ghostly domain. We
enter into it almost unwittingly, because it has no visible border" (2013,
140). The road (paved, clean, well marked) served as an eerie backdrop to
my interviews with locals and bomb technicians working in Sepon. Sitting
and chatting on people's front porches, visiting villages being cleared, or in
the training yard of a clearance operator, the road was nearly always visible
in the background. Massive trucks and off-road vehicles move fast down that
road, driving through some of the poorest districts in Laos on their way to
global markets in Vietnam, China, or Thailand.

The town of Sepon has been recentered away from the colonial ruins, in
an effort to thereby control the flow of prosperity through these mineral-
rich mountains. In recent years, as New Sepon has grown wealthier, the
flow of money and people has reversed, and Old Sepon is being renovated.
These processes engage nominally Buddhist cosmologies of urbanity and
prosperity in mainland Southeast Asia. In the cosmology at work, urbanity
may be conceived of either as sacred power, development, or culture; all extend outward and downward from a central point (Askew, Logan, and Long

2006; Johnson 2014). At the center of each city is a guardian spirit, sacred site, or monarch. Urban life is arranged to ensure the proper flow of power and prosperity from the vibrant core. A fully developed city thereby contains within it the power to incorporate the surrounding wilderness, transforming forest into wealth, barbarians into civilized people, danger into safety, or battlefields into marketplaces. "The wilderness/urban distinction [is] one of violence versus civility, chaos versus order, heat versus coolness, and ignorance versus learning" (Johnson 2014, 48). In this cosmology, Buddhism is associated with urban centers of power—the city being among the most obvious manifestations of this ability to create order from wilderness. Beginning after liberation, the Pathet Lao have manipulated this logic by recentering urban centers, such as Sepon, either by creating new socialist cities or by building new city monuments or pillars (lak, the pillar that situates guardian spirits) in established cities. But despite the regional push to create new markets where battles were once fought, in the 1990s Laos lacked the national capacity (transportation, currency, markets) to sustain such a transformation. The process of intervening into sacred centers, manipulating the logic of prosperity, was fraught from the beginning.

With the loosening of religious reforms in the last few years, the wives of the president and prime minister began leading temple and village renovation projects in Old Sepon. Together, these wives and high-ranking Party members are building new concrete buildings and a new temple, and renovating the original Wat Sepon Gao. These renovations include a massive palace, a walled concrete complex rumored to contain within it the latest in high-tech entertainment and security technologies. Taken together, these renovations are a potent demonstration of the Party elite's ability to revitalize postwar Laos by generating wealth, rebuilding communities, and supporting temples. Viewed alongside other, similar reconstruction projects, the palace complex is a specific example of a general pattern of transformative prosperity in modern Laos. Lavish houses, made out of concrete and tile, are often designed to be continually unfinished. Such houses are often built by renovating older wooden stilt houses rather than by starting afresh. Improvements, such as paint or electricity, are added through constant remodeling. Renovation is a regular process of transformation toward the ideal, toward jaleun (see introduction). It is significant that this revitalization of Sepon is staged in the ruins of the old capital rather than the newer town center—a turn from the revolutionary monument to the older Buddhist temple.

The oscillation between Old and New Sepon is a powerful indicator of the ambivalence of the Renovation project. The shift from the industrial center to the spiritual, but ruined, older center could be interpreted as an indictment of the model of progress underwriting New Sepon. At the same time, the re-centering toward Old Sepon is made possible by the money and prestige of the Renovation (and the Sepon gold mine) and is led by the highest-ranking Party members. This is a repressive, authoritarian context where the state violently positions itself as the legitimate center of national prosperity and sacred authority. The state enforces its monopoly on potential and potency: focusing on potential, rather than power, in her analysis of state authority in Laos, Sarinda Singh argues that "the state is a promise for a better future [that is] continually being constituted through the expectations and experiences of those under its authority" (2012, 155). In Sepon and elsewhere, prominent Party leaders and politicians are positioning themselves as the patrons of Laos's potency, in part by hooking the national Renovation project into local ritual revivals, thereby engaging a cosmology of prosperity that plays out through reform and revolution. The Old Sepon renovation is not a step back to a prewar era, but an effort to intervene in processes of revival that characterize contemporary Laos, thereby manipulating the production of prosperity in the service of the present regime.

Remains of War

Massive bomb craters, some twenty feet across, seemed to surround Wat Sepon Gao without touching it—but the miracle was an illusion. The temple was also destroyed during the war and later rebuilt on the same site using pieces of the original structure and other available resources. As part of the preparations for the fund-raiser to renovate the old temple, I was surprised to see local volunteers and novice monks filling in the bomb craters surrounding the temple with sand. These half-century-old craters were completely grown in with grass, shrubs, and even trees. It was a time-consuming operation since they didn't have construction equipment and must fill the craters by hand, one bag of sand at a time. Contrary to the presumed intention, the brown sand made the craters stand out against the nearly neon-green grass, bringing the curves of the bomb strike more fully into imagination. It was as if the earth had been stricken again.

The craters were filled in. Large parade awnings, with rows of folding chairs beneath, were set up on top of the craters around Wat Sepon Gao. The

FIGURE 2.3 Fifty-year-old craters used as trash pits. In the background, tables and a parking lot set up for the temple fund-raiser. Photo by the author.

day of the fund-raiser, I took a seat at the far edges of the growing crowd, in a field just outside the temple wall. While a senior monk chanted the opening prayer, a somber older man sitting next to me in the crowd began reminiscing about his childhood in Old Sepon. After the war, he told me, when his family returned to the town, one of his jobs was to collect the bombs in the field we were currently sitting in. He recalled picking up "so many, so many bombs" by hand, gathering them in a giant pile, setting the pile on fire, and then running away very fast. He gestured to a huge crater behind us, nearly overgrown with bushes, that was not filled in with sand for the event (see figure 2.3). "There was nobody to tell us how to do it, so we just did it our way." This field was now the playground of the new school rebuilt with donations from the prime minister and president. I noted the parallel of this man's memories of the field and the ritual taking place in the field. The parallel was not merely between his memories and his present experiences: the bomb craters were still here; the ruins were still here.

This experience of remains/revivals is, I argue, characteristic of how people inhabit former battlefields and interact with remains of war such as craters. The process of postwar reconstruction, even as people fill in craters

and rebuild houses, paradoxically brings the remains of war into relief. Military waste is a phenomenon that becomes more potent through the thick layering of traces; even displacement, disavowal, and discontinuity only increase its power to contaminate daily life. In the years after the war, when Laos was subject to a trade embargo, construction projects were often built using rebar, nails, and other resources made from recycled war scrap. The rebuilt Wat Sepon Gao and other similar postwar reconstruction projects are supported by the literal transformation of bombs into goods. This practice is still quite common in rural Laos, and military waste is often found as repurposed or recycled items in homes and temples. For example, the Wat Sepon Gao temple bells were made out of painted empty bomb cases (see figure 2.4). The bomb bells were donated to the temple in the name of specific individuals, often in honor of a deceased relative. It is highly likely that this set of bomb bells was donated in honor of someone who died in the war, perhaps due to the explosion of a similar type of ordnance. The inscription on the larger bomb is in Thai and records the name and location of the temple, the name of the donor, and the Buddhist calendar year 2557 (2014), meaning it was donated as part of the current temple renovation. Objects such as these bomb bells facilitate merit transfers between the living and the dead performed by monks at the temple. This is not an abstract instance of merit transfer. The bombs evocatively, sensuously, serve as conduits between the war dead and the living, and between the past bombing and the present revival. The bomb bells materially maintain their arresting associations with danger and survival: someone had to safely gather these bombs, safely disarm and dismantle them, safely handle the explosives, craft the cases into bells, paint them with the inscription, and then ritually donate them to the temple. The choice to donate bombs to the temple as ritual items materializes a process of postwar survival and revival carried out at sacred centers such as Wat Sepon Gao.

Military waste is ontologically polysemous. This feature is not unique to military waste, but I can think of few objects more ontologically arresting than an unexploded or inert bomb repurposed into a domestic good or ritual item. After Mbembe's (2013, 142) analysis of ghostly power, these repurposed military wastes have a compelling surreality—they project "a light whose starkness, harshness, and brutality invest objects, erase them, recreate them, and then plunge the subject into a quasi-hallucinatory drama" that invokes the war while simultaneously rejecting it. The transformative quality of military waste presents interesting questions about ethnographic evidence: a kind of "quasi-hallucinatory" double vision is required to see both the bomb and the temple bell at the same time. The first time that I visited Wat Sepon Gao, I was accompanied by a Lao friend of mine who worked as a bomb technician with a Sepon-based clearance operator. Wat Sepon Gao was the nearest Buddhist temple to her house, and she sometimes attended rituals at the temple. Despite her technical skills in explosives clearance, she had never noticed that the temple bells were made out of emptied bomb cases until I pointed it out to her myself. She saw her local temple; I saw that the bells were also bombs. I had, without consciously knowing it, primed myself to see double.

Toward my elaboration of a hauntology of military waste, I argue that these objects are materially haunted by the war. This argument embeds within it a methodological claim for seeing double, for seeing both the remains and revivals at the same time. My theorizing of this form of material haunting is responsive to Yael Navaro-Yashin's (2012) analysis of postwar remains in Cyprus. In her analysis, "a ghost . . . is what is retained in material objects and the physical environment" after an event; "the ghost is a thing, a material object, in itself" (2012, 17). She cultivates this analytic approach, in part, as a methodological solution to the problem of studying a war that is not absent but rather intensely present in a way that challenges conventional approaches to empirical research. This form of haunting has a material and social solidity that manifests in the ethnographic account. Research on ghosts has often inspired methodological innovation for anthropologists—a tradition of asserting ethnographic durability against assumptions that ghosts are immaterial or unreal. Inspired by Patrice Ladwig's study of ghosts in Laos, I employ the trace as a form of ethnographic evidence in my account of postwar revival: "The anthropological analysis of spirits and ghosts is situated in a field that poses basic methodological and theoretical challenges. Located in a realm that is often between visibility and invisibility, present and past, and between material and immaterial, the oscillation between these poles constitutes the framework in which the agency of spirits unfolds" (Ladwig 2013, 428). The action of ghosts and spirits is described in terms of shifts from one mode of being to another—and it is via these shifts that ghostly entities leave traces upon the world. "Traces might indicate the places where they appear, or the offerings they receive. The trace in that sense is a track, a footprint or an imprint—a sign left in the material domain of something that in conventional ways is not graspable for most people not endowed with the special capacities to do so" (Ladwig 2013, 431). Ghosts manifested a material solidity in Ladwig's ethnographic research that prompted him to reassess his empirical approach. Ladwig's framing of the trace in terms of oscillating poles is, I think, integral to understanding and researching ghostly ontologies in Laos. The bomb bells and similar repurposed military wastes are efficacious preciously because they oscillate between war and revival, danger and prosperity, the afterlife and the realm of the living. Similar to the way that filling in the craters surrounding the temple seemed to strike the ground again, the war has cultural relevance as an ongoing process of tracing and transformation. In this ghostly logic, the war was made more potent when its craters were filled in, its ruins rebuilt, and its ordnance repurposed. The bombing haunted Sepon, but also animated the town with new affects, material resources, powers, and possibilities.

The Lane Xang Gold Mine

The first half of this chapter describes the ritual renovation of Old Sepon; the second half dwells on the economic revival underwriting postwar renovation projects. My intention is to juxtapose the Old Sepon temple renovation with the economic revival occurring at New Sepon, most powerfully demonstrated by the Lane Xang gold mine. Whereas volunteers in Old Sepon are filling in the half-century-old bomb craters with sand and building on top of the French ruins, workers at the Lane Xang mine are actively excavating the earth and digging up the past. The two sites are parallel parts of a single process of postwar remains/revivals. In this and following sections, I continue to draw out a Lao political cosmology premised on intervening into cycles of revival at sacred centers (here, the Lane Xang mine). My final intent is to elaborate a hauntology: a theory of ghosts, recurring presence, and non-linear time—a theory appropriate to the Lane Xang ghost mine.

Six mining companies operate in the area surrounding Sepon, but the Lane Xang mine is the oldest and largest mine in Laos. The mine is a joint venture between MMG, a Chinese-owned Australian mining operation, and the Lao government. Explorations for the mine began in the 1990s, just as Laos was opening to foreign investors. In a paradoxical way, the successive decades of war prevented Laos's gold resources from being exploited, maintaining them for the present regime and its corporate partners. A senior mine employee commented to me that the Lane Xang mine "was really part of executing the New Economic Mechanism. There was nothing else there to help people imagine what development could be, other than the mine. . . . They saw the mine and thought of money." But fantasies of wealth were postponed for ten years, while the mine set up operations. The mine's first gold pour was in 2002 and its first copper pour in 2005. At its height in 2010–11, the mine accounted for nearly 9 percent of Laos's GDP and was the second largest employer in Laos (after the state) with more than five thousand employees (quoted in Mayes and Chang 2014). Gold production peaked at ten thousand ounces per year, before gold mining became unprofitable in late 2013. Copper production continues at about ninety thousand tons per year. Today, most of the mine's output goes toward copper cable, wires, and tubes for the Asian and European markets.

The Lane Xang mine is almost always referred to as "the gold mine," even though the mine no longer processes gold. In Laos, gold is considered superior to other forms of wealth, including currencies. Gold, often in the form of high-percentage jewelry, is easily exchangeable and is assumed to be more liquid than other forms of wealth. In this sense, gold wealth in Laos is the standard for economic transformation: underwriting personal success while also symbolically capable of transformation via markets and currency exchanges. In Laos, gold is "a common public display of relative fortune, and it is closely associated with beauty" (High 2014, 76). Referencing Marx, Holly High describes gold as something like a "chrysalis that promises the unconstrained possibility purely of becoming something else, someone else" (2014, 76). Whether proudly worn as gold jewelry or used to gild significant items, gold indicates and invites a capacity for prosperity. While "prosperity," here, refers also to social, physical, and spiritual achievements, this capacity is closely linked with economic transformation. The common title of the mine, though factually misleading, is evidence of the desires and dreams the mine enables.

Several historical strata are being dug up at the mine: its title refers to the fourteenth-century kingdom of Lane Xang Hom Khao (Land of a Million Elephants and the White Parasol), usually represented as the national progenitor of the Lao state. The kingdom of Lane Xang immediately predates Siamese conquest and French colonialism of the region. The name of the mine is a symbolic return to a mythical, fully independent Laos untarnished by war, colonialism, or imperialism. As with the Wat Sepon Gao renovation, the use of prewar motifs is not an indictment of the present regime but a revival of older forms in the service of future imagined prosperity. The title of the mine has lately become a reference to the richness of archaeological artifacts found during mining operations. These archaeological finds have also raised the status of the mine in the eyes of the regime: "The government loves it [artifacts] because it is evidence . . . of their culture going back thousands of years," a mine employee comments to me. Things being dug up at the mine may be used to legitimate present social and economic transformation by demonstrating continuity with Laos's golden age. Bronze Age artifacts excavated from the mine are proudly presented at regional and national museums as evidence of a continuous Lao presence at the site. Archaeological excavations at the mine have uncovered evidence of copper mining as far back as 2,300 years (Mayes and Chang 2014).

More recent strata include the site's history of being a Pathet Lao communist stronghold during the Vietnam-American War. The gold mine is built directly on top of a major meeting point along the Ho Chi Minh Trail, one of the most bombed parts of all Indochina. The literal transformation of the

Pathet Lao camp into a gold mine is a potent symbol of the Party's potential to generate wealth for the country, to be literally the fount of gold. At the same time, the site remains massively contaminated with dangerous, live ordnance—an ambivalent legacy waiting to be dug up. "How many bombs were dug up for every ounce of gold?" I asked one of the managers of the mine. To date, the mine operators have destroyed more than 45,000 items of unexploded ordnance (MMG 2016). The bombs are literally destroyed, demolished, while the gold is carefully cataloged and weighed to the ounce. Bomb clearance has been routinized into mining operations at the Lane Xang mine from the very beginning, predating the first mining activities. In this sense, the mine did not begin with gold, or with Party zeal; I am told by a mine worker that "the mine began with [bomb] clearance." Literally, the first things to be dug up at the mine were bombs unearthed and demolished in the initial construction. The mine employs its own in-house, full-time clearance team; in addition, they may hire private contract clearance teams as needed. The mine's clearance teams have found ordnance every working day since operations began in 2002. Large air-drop bombs have been found pummeled into the earth as deep as twelve meters.

The Sepon Ghost Mine

I first heard the phrase "ghost mine" while doing site visits and interviews with an explosives clearance operator in Sepon. I was traveling with my interpreter to a village known for its war scrap trading. Our plan was to interview local scrap traders about their work, safety practices, and perceptions of military waste. This village had been previously cleared by an official clearance operator, but remained a nexus for regional war scrap trading. The surrounding area was rich in ordnance and other battleground wastes such as helmets and gear. The village lay along the paved road that leads out of New Sepon to the gold mine. Several of the houses had concrete rooms or understories, well maintained but unpainted—funded by jobs at the mine. We pulled our car up to the chief's house, a large wooden stilt house whose broad porch fronted the paved road. We intended only to introduce ourselves as a perfunctory gesture before interviewing residents, but wound up spending several hours sitting on the porch talking with the chief and his wife. The chief proudly told us that this was a "majority Buddhist village." It turned out that the chief and his wife were scrap traders. The wife was also a laborer at the gold mine.

FIGURE 2.5 The author handling an inert BLU-3 on display at COPE Visitor Centre, Vientiane. Photo by Jill Martinucci, used with permission.

She very quickly monopolized the conversation, telling me successively more terrible stories of deadly explosions in the village, speaking with thinly veiled anger and sadness. As the stories continued, it became clear to me that her brother died in a cluster bomb explosion when they were children. These were her stories, and stories of her friends and family. I was struck by the ferocity of her speech, as the norm in Laos is to let difficult topics lie still and undisturbed. I had introduced myself as a "researcher studying bomb culture" (*wattanatam giogab labeurd*), and it occurred to me that she wanted me to record her stories in my notes.

In between stories, the chief briefly entered the house and returned with a matched set of dismantled BLU-3s, a type of cluster submunition commonly called "pineapple bombs" (*laberd maak nad*) for their resemblance to the spiked fruit (see figure 2.5). These bombs are yellow with a large crown of metal fins. This pair had been converted into matched ashtrays, painted red. He offered the bombs to me, cupped in his palms like halved fruit.

I took one. It was surprisingly heavy, even empty. The opening at the top of the ashtray (the bottom of the bomb) was only a few inches across. The rut for the screw cap was still visible around the edge of the opening. The outer wall was textured by tiny balls of shrapnel.

"When I found it," he said, "it was rusty brown. So I painted it red . . . to remind me to tell my children not to touch bombs if they find them."

"In America, red is the color of danger," I replied.

Using these props, the two of them demonstrated how to dismantle a BLU-3 by hand. The chief's wife took one and pretended to grip the fins in one fist, while firmly holding the base of the bomb in her other hand. With the fins up, she said, the bomb cannot trigger. Carefully, with her other hand, she fiddled with the pin that secures the cap on the base of the bomb. If she couldn't get the bottom to open on its own, she could use a rock to deform the thin metal cap. Once the cap was off, the explosive was revealed and could be easily removed. Finally, she deftly twisted the bomb: fins in one direction, the base in another. "We do it like this."

My interpreter helped me follow along with this display of skill. "There are many bombs in the river. The ghost mine—"

I interrupted. "Ghost mine? What is that?"

My interpreter clarified: "Ghost mine . . . ghost . . . I mean *gold* mine. . . . She says that the gold mine is using a high-power water jet to remove part of the mountain and that this puts all of the bombs [in the mountain] in the river. She finds many bombs by the river." Such as these two.

My interpreter's slip between "ghost" and "gold" was very apt, and the phrase "ghost mine" stuck with us for a long time after our visit to that village. Drawing on Catherine Malabou's treatise on explosive accidents, Carolyn Shread (Malabou's translator) examines word accidents as the condition of possibility for all translations: "Much as we wish for a translation that would never trip up, a translation lying seamlessly next to its source, to take on a translation is to take on the accident" (2012, ix). Accident, for Malabou and Shread, refers to the generative power of catastrophe to produce new and unexpected forms.

In the explosives clearance sector, "accident" generally refers to the explosion of ordnance after the end of conflict that causes injury to a person or persons (see my discussion of accident in the introduction). Like Ernst Jünger in his military science fiction novel *The Glass Bees*, quoted in the epigraph to this chapter via Gilles Deleuze and Félix Guattari's discussion of the war machine, I understand accidents as "optical illusions" that obscure the process of war and military wasting. Jünger writes, "It is an optical illusion to attribute these [war-related] mutilations to accidents. Actually, accidents are the result of mutilations that took place long ago in the embryo of our world. . . . The loss occurred long before it was visibly taken into account" (Jünger 1957, 112, quoted in Deleuze and Guattari 1987, 426). Deleuze and Guattari expand on Jünger's comments, asserting that imperial warfare "needs . . . predisposable people, preexisting amputees" selected for injury in advance (1987, 426). The very term "accident" feels deceptive—a disavowal of a half century of violent consequences of the Vietnam-American War. Nonetheless, and in spite of my careful refusal of the language of accident, the term remained a potent nexus of research. Following Jünger's insight to treat accidents as optical illusions that obscure imperial violence, I wondered what else was obscured by the language of the accident: Just as military waste exceeds the conditions of an originating conflict, might ordnance explosions also exceed the violence of war? And how might one learn to recognize this potential—to see through the optical illusion? Thinking beyond war and the aims of military strategists, what are the accidental consequences of ordnance explosions?

My translator's trip-up between "gold" and "ghost" unintentionally expanded my own thinking about accidents in my research. Like Malabou (2012, 4) and Shread (2012), I found myself thinking about "the plastic art of destruction" as it has unexpectedly, and repeatedly, transformed my research and methodology throughout this project. The gold mine/ghost mine parallel involved a kind of accidental translation: the mine laborer's phrase ("gold mine") and the translator's phrase ("ghost mine") do not lie seamlessly next to each other, but form a generative parallel that I expand and examine in this chapter. It was rare for me to hear ghosts openly discussed in an interview or site visit—though the topic was common late-night conversation in less formal settings. Andrew A. Johnson, working in Thailand, remarks that "the topic of ghosts was either extremely easy or essentially impossible to broach" and many interlocutors "took great pains to disavow [ghosts] in the face of the foreign researcher" (2014, 303). This was especially true in Laos, where there was extreme pressure to craft accounts for researchers that were in line with the official discourse of modernization, absent what the state categorized as superstition. This disavowal of ghosts constitutes another example of hazardous data, whereby I adapted my data collection methods to be sensitive to absences, refusals, and silences (see my discussion of thin description in the introduction). My translator's use of "ghost" unexpectedly invited the possibility of ghosts into the mine laborer's conversation about bombs, death, and misfortune. I could, essentially, hear the ghosts that were not being discussed. Having thus heard a ghost, I showed that I was receptive to the topic by remarking on the mistranslation in a positive light (without derision for superstition), and by displaying open body language. Responding positively to the mistranslation, the mine laborer took up my unvoiced invitation and proceeded to tell me about ghosts in the area. In conversations such as this one, I was learning how to hear and invite what people were not openly willing to say.

The Lane Xang mine, by the very nature of mining in massively contaminated areas, is digging up bombs and may be spreading bombs, via the runoff, into local communities. I was not able to confirm fears of bomb runoff with my interlocutors at the mine. The mine company has an official policy of being "zero harm, fatality free," and management takes pride in the mine's excellent safety record. Regardless of its veracity, the assertion that the gold mine is producing bombs and ghosts is revealing in and of itself. These assertions by mine workers constitute another kind of ethnographic trace—evidence that exists between states, neither verified nor unverified, but clearly significant. Haunting operates on a different kind of empiricism, one that is rooted in our body's senses, but that feels what is present as much as what is absent; not seeing a ghost can make a haunting feel more intense rather than less. Ghost stories do not propagate on conventionally empirical, verifiable evidence (which, as I noted earlier, does not at all diminish their significance as ethnographic evidence). In this sense, the mine may produce ghosts regardless of whether there are bombs in the runoff.

In our discussion with the chief and his wife who worked at the mine, victims, such as the wife's brother who died in a cluster bomb explosion, were referred to as victims of "unnatural death," a euphemism for angry ghosts (phi dtai hong). These kinds of ghosts are extremely dangerous because they may threaten and even kill people out of vengeance for their own death, with a vicious attention to those that were close to them in life. Particularly violent events may have repercussions for decades afterward—entailments that generate more violence unless angry ghosts are appeased. In this way, the living may become entangled in relations with the violently dead. In their separate examinations of the haunting of postwar Vietnam, Heonik Kwon (2008) and Mai Lan Gustafsson (2009) both demonstrate that these spiritual relations may manifest in the bodies of the living as violent possessions, illness, bad luck, and death. Gustafsson describes the postwar period of the Vietnam-American War as "the age of wild ghosts" (2009, 70). Ongoing violence due to military waste explosions continually arrests people's abilities to correctly memorialize the dead and stave off further cyclical violence. Bomb explosions are often understood to be set off by angry ghosts, with the ghosts themselves generally having been past victims of the war and its waste. The mine laborer's stories dwelt on the community's efforts to reduce the potentially deadly consequences of these unnatural, violent deaths.

She described a recent explosion: A family of three brothers, all specialists in dismantling and trading bombs, scouted a large general-purpose bomb in the jungle. In the morning, the three of them headed out into the jungle to dismantle the bomb. Meanwhile, she was in a truck with the other wage laborers, heading to the gold mine for work.

"I hear a really big boom, and we think, 'Oh, that is them!' and all three are just gone!" She waved her hands loosely, a gesture meant to be taken by the wind. "With the big bomb, all that is left to find is an arm. We don't know who it is, but we bury it in the jungle. And do a spirit call back in the village."

Alerted by the sound of the blast, the village chief (her husband) sent a group to the site of the explosion. Only a single arm out of three brothers was recoverable. General-purpose bombs are among the most valuable kinds of ordnance in the scrap market. A general-purpose bomb in Laos can be quite large, ranging from 250 pounds to as much as 2,000 pounds. Each bomb is designed to kill people and destroy an area through a large blast and fragmentation outward from the point of impact or detonation. In such an event, anyone within the immediate blast zone would be instantly, and completely, obliterated.

She went on to describe how the corpses of victims are handled by the community: "They don't know who is who and then they get the monks to call back the spirit. . . . They don't want to bring the unnatural dead back into the village because they worry that it will cause other accidents. But bringing it to the temple is safe."

It was too dangerous to bring the bodies back into the village, especially in this case since only a single arm was recoverable. The brothers had no other relatives to conduct proper burial rites, or receive the spirits when they were called back. All three were doomed to wander as ghosts, potential sources of further misfortune for the community. The general-purpose bomb was both the cause and the result of misfortune for the brothers and the community as a whole. The site of an explosion may become haunted by the ghost of the victim, who in turn may trigger further deadly explosions. Each explosion is thus potentially part of a cycle of violence, connected to other explosions, injuries, and deaths in the village. In the present tense, Gustafsson writes in her study of postwar Vietnam that the war is "infusing millions of fresh souls into the spirit world, and relegating millions more to a hellish status as wandering ghosts" (2009, xiii). Together, sitting on the chief's porch, the four of us go over what an explosion could mean: any one explosion may indicate the presence of a spirit at that site who triggered the blast, or that the spirit of the victim has been caught at that site and needs to be called back before it kills others passing by. In either case, for Buddhist communities, monks and other local spiritual leaders can intervene into cycles of violence by propitiating ghosts and calling back spirits.

"We Mine for Progress"

The Lane Xang mining company's primary goal, as explained by two anthropologists hired by the mine as cultural resource experts, is "to realise the value of things in the ground by transforming them into commodity and capital and as a consequence generating extraordinary social change" (Mayes and Chang 2014, 240). Mine employees are part of an ongoing process of transforming "things in the ground," producing value out of what is buried. The mine company's slogan proclaims, "We Mine for Progress." I identify this version of progress, after Rosalind Williams's analysis of underground imaginaries, as "the advancement of knowledge and the conquest of external nature" (2008, 204). In Williams's analysis of technological progress, mining operations are prototypical examples of highly technologized, purely human-built environments that succeed via mastery over nature. Massive military waste subverts this logic of progress by upending the distinction between human-built and natural environments, or, more profoundly, the distinction between technological progress and destruction. Rather, technological progress has transformed the ground itself into a highly militarized, hazardous zone. What is actually "in the ground" at the mine? As my discussion of the ghost mine in the previous sections indicates, more than gold is being uncovered and transformed at the mine.

Warren Mayes and Nigel Chang (2014), an anthropologist and an archaeologist (respectively) employed at the Lane Xang mine, describe the recurring spirit possessions at the mine. Shortly after the first discovery of archaeological artifacts at the mine, staff reported hearing cries coming from the dig site. The next morning, the mine sponsored a spirit ceremony to address the spirits in the pit, asking permission to proceed with excavations. During this period, one of the local staff members was possessed by the spirit of an elderly man named Uncle Pouan. "The possession was physical and emotional, the employee's body shaking, tears streaming, as witnessed and video-recorded on the mobile phone of another employee" (Mayes and Chang 2014, 239). Uncle Pouan was an inhabitant of the ancient village being uncovered by mining operations. He was upset that excavations had not ceased immediately upon the discovery of the remains of his village. The possessed person reported dreams of Uncle Pouan's village: small bamboo and grass-thatched huts climbing the side of the mountain. Uncle Pouan walked through the dream village, carrying a bamboo staff (239). The mine employees were successful in placating Uncle Pouan, who departed during the spirit ceremony, and received spiritual permission to continue excavations. The possessed employees were subsequently interviewed by mine and government officials for details about the dig site. The visitation by Uncle Pouan was not an isolated incident; other possession events involved Uncle Pouan and his son.

The request for spiritual permission was not only directed at Uncle Pouan and the ancient village that he represented, but was also a request by local staff to participate "on their own terms by authorizing the discovery" of archaeological artifacts (Mayes and Chang 2014, 240). An archaeologist working at the site during the period of spirit possessions described the ancient village to me as a "strata of spirits. . . . These are the unintended implications of archaeology—the digging up disturbs spirits." Mayes and Chang contend that the possession and ceremony was "an alternative source of 'ownership participation' linking ancient heritage with contemporary local user rights and a desire for inclusion in the story of mining development" (240). Whenever mine management requests access to a new site, mine employees negotiate with local land users and elders, who in turn negotiate with territorial or ancestral spirits residing at the site. Spirit mediums offer spirits food and other sacrifices donated by the mining company for this purpose. Participation in local ownership rituals is encouraged by mine management in order to prevent the mine being blamed for local calamities. A senior mine employee explains to me, "There are spirits here, and it is important that we publicly acknowledge that and worry about it."

Though spirit possession is generally seen as superstition, antithetical to official government plans for development, these possession events were actively discussed by mine and government staff. Most local staff at the mine belong to the Phou Tai and Mon Khmer ethnic groups, and most mining sites in Sepon are in areas glossed by the government and mining officials as ethnic minority areas. In official discourse, this phrase indicates cultural, religious, and agricultural practices that differ from those of the ruling, lowland Lao elite.* In an area where non-Lao practices, especially non-Lao Buddhist religious practices, are often hidden from official view, the prominence of the spirit possessions at the mine was remarkable. These unusual meetings between mine officials, local minority groups, and spirits were partially the result of official mine policies. The Lane Xang mine pursues a policy of local engagement, activities that include hiring and training local staff, sponsoring religious events related to the mine, creating a cultural heritage center, and hiring anthropologists to study local communities. The discovery of archaeological artifacts by mine workers has inspired visits by leading Lao officials, including the prime minister. Communities and practices that might normally be sidelined (a category in which I include local ghosts and spirits) are instead invited to participate at high-profile events. Policies of local engagement have enabled the participation of non-Lao ethnic groups at the very center of economic revival in Sepon.

The mine pursues local engagement practices in order "to understand and manage the risk that impacts on the surrounding communities may lead to significant disruption of mining operations" (Mayes and Chang 2014, 238). I point this out not as a cynic, but to highlight how danger and risk permeate the search for wealth at the mine. The mainstreaming of clearance at the mine arises out of this same paradigm of risk mitigation; clearance, cultural heritage, and spirit possession are intertwined risk practices. Partially to reduce the risk of bomb explosions at the mine, local staff were encouraged to speak up if they found "signs of prior disturbance" in the soil (239). Mine management set up incentive programs to encourage staff to literally keep their eyes on the ground, looking for and reporting any explosive ordnance or archaeological artifacts they find. Mining operations, explosives

---

* The are no stable definitions of ethnicity in Laos (e.g., in a national census), meaning that the phrase "ethnic minority" has incredible mobility and polysemy on the ground, and yet always implicitly references a default Lao national ethnicity. Demographically, the Lao elite are also a minority in many areas; non-Lao "majority-minorities" constitute at least 90 percent of the population in several provinces (Cooper 2014, 81). I include the phrase "ethnic minority" in my analysis as ethnographic evidence of how these communities are discussed by the state and its development partners.

clearance, and archaeological research are intertwined in a subterranean ontology—each, in their own way, focuses downward in order to dig up and destroy.

Williams remarks that mines provoke a "subterranean consciousness— the awareness that we are in a very real sense not on the earth but inside it" (Williams 2008, 212–13). At the Lane Xang mine, this sense of being inside a militarized subterranean environment subverts the narrative of extracting resources from an external nature: it is as if, instead of digging for gold, the miners are suddenly instead digging trenches for an endless war. The onto-logical focus on "things in the ground" is warped. There is no escape route, no way out of this militarized terrain. I align this subterranean ontology with Williams's theory of a Cold War imaginary characterized by war trenches, bomb shelters, and underground military waste depositories. In this Cold War imaginary, "military and ecological security have converged" under-ground (Williams 2008, 208); or, rephrased for my research, military and ecological insecurity have converged underground. Mines are prototypes of technologized progress over nature. Mines are also prototypical examples of the subversion of progress—the terror of being buried alive when the tech-nological apparatus of a mine (excavations, drainage, ventilation, lighting, etc.) fails.

These ancestral and territorial spirits are not merely being unearthed at the mine; they are being unearthed by the miners in the course of routine mining operations. Mining itself—the act of realizing the value of what is in the ground—unexpectedly intersects with many kinds of buried things (gold, copper, military waste, ancient artifacts, ghosts, and spirits). Digging up the gold also involves digging up troubling or politically sensitive pasts. Mining has, accidentally, became a process of resurrection. I take these ac-counts of spirit possession by territorial or ancestral spirits unearthed by miners as important evidence of ongoing local intervention into cycles of war/revival in Sepon. Mine laborers and officials may be exhibiting what High (2014, 150) refers to as "the desiring resurrection of the state," here exemplified by the literal resurrection of artifacts and spirits from Laos's pre-war, precolonial past. As High describes with regard to failed poverty reduc-tion projects in southern Laos: "The state is constantly resurrected despite the demolitions it is subject to in everyday disgruntlement, distrust and suspicion. Even when demands for state largesse [remain] often unfulfilled, and themselves become the source of disgruntlement, the fantasy remains, and is indeed intensified. The state haunts even those who reject it most forcibly—and this capacity for resurrection and return is one of the key characteristics of desire itself" (2014, 124).

The Lane Xang mine, a dual government-corporate operation, demonstrates the effectiveness of the Lao state's promises of future prosperity, promises that may only become more compelling as they remain unfulfilled. The desire and the ruin remain, perhaps especially for ethnic minority communities generally sidelined by Lao development policy. The ancient kingdom of Lane Xang is transformed by mining operations into a possible force for renewal, a spirit from the past harnessed to sanction economic reforms and positively intervene into cycles of misfortune. This is not to say that the process is unambiguously positive. Instead of a historical logic, a kind of ghostly logic is in play: events layer themselves thinly, characterized by unexpected subterranean returns and the possibility of digging something, or someone, out of the earth.

Mining operations at the Lane Xang mine will likely end by 2020. Gold mining ended in 2013, and copper mining is swiftly becoming unprofitable as well. A senior mining executive explains, "It is a business—MMG has mines from the DRC to Peru. There are other parts of this business. When mines close in one area . . ." He balances his hands up and down, indicating that when one mine closes down, a new mine opens in another area. From the company's point of view, the Lane Xang mine is part of a business cycle premised on the closure and opening of mines. Each mine has a life cycle that can be calculated using site surveys, the cost of production, and the price of metals. Global markets are presently experiencing a downturn in the price of copper, meaning that excavations and explorations in Sepon are no long supportable by profits from the mine alone. At the same time, the Lao government maintains a moratorium on new mining operations while it responds to complaints of corruption and exploitation of local communities by some mine operations (not at the Lane Xang gold mine). What ghosts will the abandoned Lane Xang mine leave behind in the soil?

A Hauntology of Military Waste

The prevalence of spirits and ghosts not only is an object of inquiry, but also invites a mode of inquiry. What is happening in Sepon, at the ghost mine and in the surrounding area, is "haunting rather than 'history'" (Gordon 2008, 142). Bombs and other ordnance from a war that ended forty years ago describe a history that is out of joint; bombs are "not docile to time" (Derrida

[1993] 2006, xix). Mine laborers and others are learning "to live with ghosts" (Derrida [1993] 2006, xviii). The haunting of Sepon begins in "the untimeliness of its present," a particularly potent remark for thinking about military waste persisting decades after conflict in Laos (Derrida [1993] 2006, 202). And yet, Sepon does not appear to be a bombed-out ruin: the Lane Xang gold mine is an active mine, recently built, with new equipment and staff; the town is experiencing a construction boom; the old, destroyed capital is being repopulated and rebuilt.

A bomb technician working in Sepon, who herself grew up in a different contaminated province, told me during my fieldwork for this chapter, "People decided to end the war in 1975, but it didn't end. People are still *dying* and the bombs are still *here*." In my analysis, hauntology is not merely a theoretical frame, nor are the ghosts merely metaphorical. The war does not haunt like a ghost. The war haunts, in the form of material remains, ongoing violence, spirit possessions, endangered lives, resurrected pasts, and contaminated futures. How might I theorize ghosts in accord with my ethnographic evidence—not as conceptual metaphor, or existential quandary, but as real phenomena? I understand hauntology as a description of ghostly relationships that pertain in postwar zones, not of particular hauntings that compel an existentially real afterlife. These phenomena are rooted in specific mainland Southeast Asian conceptions of haunting, while also being linked to shared experiences of war and military wasting that cross ethnic and religious communities—contributing to a general theory of postwar haunting. Following Navaro-Yashin (2012), I have pursued a method of attention toward the haunting material remains of war. And, after Patrice Ladwig (2013), I have applied an ethnographic method of traces to identify these ghostly phenomena as they unevenly manifest. Engaging with local ghost stories is another intuitive way to examine ghosts as real cultural phenomena. I respond to these problems particular to studying ghosts by reworking the relations between evidence and perception, provoking a form of empiricism attuned to traces, or oscillations between the present and the absent.

The cultural and sociopolitical reality of ghosts does not lack material veracity or rigor; nor does ethnographic engagement with ghosts compel belief in a religious afterlife. On this point, I steer a different tack from many theorists who take up the idea of the ghost as a "conceptual metaphor" for understanding contemporary issues (del Pilar Blanco and Peeren 2013, 9). I quibble with the hair-splitting assertion that "spectrality does not involve the conviction that ghosts exist" (Jameson 1999, 39). If not ghosts, then what?

What other entity possesses such disturbing and uncanny abilities to puncture the present? The study of ghosts is marred by the question of existential evidence (and angst). Derrida: "[The ghost] must not exist, therefore we have to get rid of it, therefore we have to be done with it. Here you have a 'therefore' that would already be enough to rattle good sense from the inside. For if there is no such thing, why would we have to chase after the specter, to chase it out or hunt it down?" (Derrida and Stiegler 2013, 44–45). Ghosts haunt scholarship itself.

Inspired by Derrida's hauntology, and probably equally frustrated by the theory's elusiveness, Avery Gordon (2008) explores haunting as it underpins knowledge production. The existential reality of an afterlife is irrelevant to her (and my) analysis. For Gordon, experiences of being haunted demand theories and methods attuned to ghostly phenomena, generally understood to be outside conventional modes of inquiry. Gordon describes haunting as "an animated state in which a repressed or unresolved social violence is making itself known" (2008, xvi). Haunting changes our experience of being in time, juxtaposing the present with problematic pasts. More precisely, ghosts are social phenomena that manifest because of the inevitable incompleteness of repression and containment. This applies to academic knowledge production as well: ghosts are equally resistant to evidence and certainty in scholarship. Ghosts are entities that don't fit the given temporality but remain persistently present; in this case, a narrative of postwar progress and national development. Bruno Latour describes modern temporality as a process that represses some histories and not others: "Modern temporality is the result of a retraining imposed on entities which would pertain to all sorts of times and possess all sorts of ontological statuses without this harsh disciplining" (1993, 72). In this understanding of time, ghosts are quintessential figures of globalization. They arise at points of friction between histories and regimes, marking the presence or absence of "disciplining." Quite literally, Laos's ghosts are traces of a silenced present, victims of a war that still remains officially secret even as its explosive ordnance continues to maim and kill.

Hauntology is notoriously difficult to engage with theoretically; I say this without critique, as this is certainly one of its strengths. Julian Wolfreys writes that "for Derrida, the spectral is a concept without a concept. . . . Spectrality resists conceptualization" (2013, 70) precisely because it continually haunts itself with what cannot be neatly conceptualized. The ghost is crafted out of its own negation (neither alive nor dead) and is not defined by any kind of resolution. Like other authors before me, I find this irreducibility theoretically fruitful: "Conversing with spectres is not undertaken in the expectation that they will reveal some secret, shameful or otherwise. Rather, it may open us up to the experience of secrecy as such: an essential unknowing which underlies and may undermine what we think we know" (Davis 2013, 56). An "experience of secrecy" and an "essential unknowing" are both topics I have already taken up in chapter 1, in the context of my discussion of methods for hazardous research. The practice of Lao parallelism, which I discussed in that chapter, vivifies my own reading of Derrida's hauntology. His hauntology examines the tension "between two, and between all the 'two's' one likes, such as between life and death," and how this tension "can only maintain itself with some ghost" ([1993] 2006, xvii). The neither/nor relation of Derrida's hauntology does not necessarily map onto Lao notions of parallelism; there is a need to further theorize hauntology away from its Judeo-Christian roots in France, Britain, and the United States. I assert the reality of ghosts against the tendency in the spectral turn to engage Judeo-Christian afterlives and, in particular, Gothic forms of haunting to the exclusion of other forms. Much of my fieldwork data seems to exist between parallel statements, sites, or experiences (such as the parallels between Old and New Sepon, or between the gold mine and the ghost mine, which I am laying out in the present chapter). Parallels come in pairs but are not necessarily oppositionally or dialectically related. There is no expectation of resolution—only a seemingly empty space, a generative gap, between the two.

Methodologically, allowing oneself to be haunted may be a crucial way to understand sensitive, silenced phenomena. In their studies of postwar Vietnam, Gustafsson (2009) and Kwon (2008) speculate that the increasing presence of spirits and ghosts is a direct effect of past wars and ongoing violence in mainland Southeast Asia. In this Lao regional cosmology, when one is possessed by a ghost the most appropriate response is to learn the identity and history of the ghost, usually with the assistance of a medium. With that knowledge, the possessed may soothe and exorcise the ghost in the most appropriate way. Sometimes, merely completing the ghost's story is enough to facilitate an exorcism. The accidental translation of the gold/ghost mine might be read as a scholarly exorcism in which I was learning to hear a repressed history. My own experiences of being haunted by the war inspire, and continue to inspire, my research. I must be both the anthropologist and the exorcist: actively listening for the ghost in the gold mine.

Conclusion: Whose Paradise?

The door of the ruined French bank vault in Old Sepon was removed from, or blown off, its hinges long ago. The vault itself was impressive: it retained its four, foot-thick walls lined with slim wooden shelves, a floor carpeted in rubble. The plaster on the inner walls had been taken over by skeins of black mold and fuzzy moss. It smelled like decomposing leaves or musty paper. I scanned the floor, noticed plastic snack wrappers. My interlocutor went further in, toward the back wall.

"I wonder if there is any money left," she playfully said.

Miraculously, she found a modern five hundred kip note (about six cents USD) on a back shelf held down by a rock. Many small rocks had been placed, or had fallen, on the shelves. The kip note was coated in black mold and was nearly unrecognizable. A putrescent deposit generating interest. "But it is modern Lao money—not old enough. We should put it back."

All the money in the vault was gone—all that remained was worthless, the unfulfilled promise of wealth. Where did the money go? A few steps away from the moldering vault, Wat Sepon Gao was being magnificently renovated. The temple fund-raiser was wildly successful, raising over 400,000,000 kip (about fifty thousand USD), far more than what was needed for the budgeted renovations. And a few steps in the other direction, prominent Party wives were building a whole new temple, and beyond that lay the president's massive walled palace complex with the latest amenities. It appeared that the money was coming back, through circuitous paths. Prior to the building of the gold mine, much of Sepon was reachable only by wet season boat. Communities that, a few years ago, gathered most of their goods and foods from the forest are now hooked into regional and global economies. The villages surrounding the mine were sustained by mining jobs, and provided with electricity, markets, running water, roads, and public buses to the provincial capital. At the same time, otherwise isolated highland, generally Phou Tai and Mon Khmer, communities were more likely to be negatively impacted by mining and logging activities, while also being less likely to directly receive benefits (Mayes and Chang 2014).

The cycle of remains/revival that I have been examining in this chapter also implies the repetition of the vices of prior regimes. When a friend learned that I would soon be traveling to Sepon, he laughed: "Savannakhet means paradise, because there is a lot of gold there. But who is the gold for? The foreigners." He was from Savannakhet but was not able to secure his future in that province. The gold was never meant for him. He recently moved to Vientiane to increase his income as a tuk-tuk driver. I was one of his foreigner fares, a reliable source of good rates.

Contemporary economic reforms have not been accompanied by significant increases in civil freedoms, democratization, or other liberal values. There has been no significant lessening of Party influence or dispersion of wealth beyond the elite. For many, Savannakhet has become a symbol of immoral and misguided wealth, the paradise that isn't what it appears: "If you want to buy paradise, go to *Savannakhet*. But if you do, you will not go to paradise [*savan*]," a monk remarked humorously in a holy day sermon I attended.

This uncertainty about the forward motion of Sepon helps to contextualize temple renovations such as the Wat Sepon Gao fund-raiser, as well as the spirit resurrections occurring at the mine. Both spirit mediums and developers appear to be working toward the same goal, that is, the revitalization of ruins. In the northern Thai context, Johnson (2014) analyzes how urban planning, development, and spirit mediumship share the concept of the city, or sacred center, being the vehicle through which prosperity is secured or ruined. Particularly as conventional sites of development become haunted by ghosts, "[spirit] possession becomes a source of potential" for revitalizing sacred centers in decline (Johnson 2014, 154). The rise of ghosts and spirit mediumship in mainland Southeast Asia, widely remarked upon by contemporary scholars, is for Johnson (2014) a sign of widespread doubt concerning conventional forms of development (see Klima 2002; Ladwig 2013; Tanabe 2002). The ghosts that haunt the Lane Xang gold mine and other sites of economic activity were seen as evidence of the weakening of the sacred center, while also being the potential means to revivify that center. Possessing spirits and haunting ghosts shared demands with reformers and developers: the demand for revival.

This parallel process of remains/revival was implicit in Sepon's post-conflict landscape, the target of both bombing raids and economic reform. Military waste has the insidious, mobile ability to cross-cut war and peace— arguably, a designed feature of large-scale, intensive cluster bombing. Writing on the air war in Laos, Fred Branfman (2013, 25) uses U.S. government reports to demonstrate that the military goal of the bombings was to destroy social and economic infrastructure, foreclosing any possibility of a strong socialist state. Postwar reconstruction and development were haunted before the war ended. It is especially important to study the lived legacies of air wars because cluster bombs and associated ordnance were intended to have lingering, socially disruptive effects. Development often carries this other side, a dark face. Rosalind Williams, after Michael Barkun's study of disaster, analyzes the simultaneity of destruction and progress. Destruction, understood "as a long-term, fundamental destruction of the primary environment" (Williams 2008, 201) is necessarily a component of progress. Mountains are razed and inverted into mines; the earth is literally blasted and shaken. Physical and social systems break down as new systems are built in their place: "Progress is destruction" (201).

My Vientiane neighbors warned me that ghosts and spirits wandered our village at night—I should be careful and listen for the sounds of dogs, who can see ghosts better than humans can. These wandering spirits were the result of the rapid transformation of the village as it was incorporated into the urban downtown. Territorial spirits were being uprooted by new concrete buildings, corporate offices, shopping malls, and hotels. The owners of these new buildings apparently failed to properly respect the territorial spirits that already lived there. Development digs up, or uproots, things that were buried, thereby producing the conditions for its own haunting. Increased traffic caused deadly road accidents, raising the number of angry ghosts on the streets. In my neighborhood, the newly built shopping mall was the tallest building, literally overshadowing older wooden houses and newer concrete apartment complexes (like the one I lived in). The neon glow from the mall's massive sign cast colored, disembodied shadows that walked the wet streets, visible for blocks in all directions. Dogs barked at night as the ghosts passed by.

FIELDPOEM 23
Blast Radius

This space and
all precious beings

Searchers use bullhorns to shock the cows
from the yellow sapless field

I imagine the birds going dumb inside it
falling from the sky

At the safe point on the far side of this pepper tree
"He holds the wire from his box of nerves
Praising mortal error"*

Premonition flattens my view
Startled by birds

I listen to the hushing wind—
This space and nothing

* A reference to other war poems (Thomas [1953] 2013).

3 • BLAST RADIUS

———

To be listening is always to be on the edge of meaning,
or in an edgy meaning of extremity, as if the sound were precisely
nothing else than its edge, this fringe, this margin—
—JEAN-LUC NANCY, *On Listening* (2007)

To someone who has never felt a bomb, bomb is only a word.
—PAT FRANK, introduction to *Alas, Babylon* (2013)

Prelude: Demolition

"One, two, three, go!"

The bomb technician triggered the controlled demolition. There was a
moment of listening silence as the signal was transmitted from the technician's trigger mechanism to the rigged C4 explosives. Then I felt the front
of a shockwave and heard a deep, low boom. At the safe point four hundred
meters from the demolition pit, behind tree cover, we did not have a direct
line of sight to the explosion but could readily hear and feel the blast. This
particular boom was anechoic; there were no nearby mountains or large
buildings to multiply and amplify the sound of the explosion. Massively,
the sound rustled its way through fields of brittle grasses that continued to

shake in all directions for some time after the demolition. The sound disturbed bamboo houses, local residents watching from afar, the fences of pig pens, meandering cows, vegetable gardens, dry rice paddies, small copses of trees, and a dusty dirt road. Even in the sonic shadow of a large pepper tree four hundred meters away, I felt the cool blast of the shockwave pushing me backward, passing through me. I stood still while the sound filled me, and for a fraction of a second, replaced the thumping of my heart and my breath in my chest. My hair and shirt fluttered against and behind my body. Trees clamored and a ruckus of soil, leaves, and other detritus briefly saturated the air with the smell of turned earth. The blast occupied the plain and was shaped by its features. It is hard to describe sounds, but if thunder snaps, like a whip long and narrow, then this explosion bloomed or rippled outward, and was spherical and densely textured. The sound sort of crackled a bit around the edges and seemed to break in the air and dissolve at some distance far behind and above me.

Only once the sound had diminished to the rustle of the grasses and the trees did I notice that one of the clearance staffers had fallen to the ground trembling with his hands over his head. He was a Lao office worker, not a bomb technician, visiting this clearance site as part of the review of the field office accounts. This was his first explosion and his first demolition. I noted my standing stillness in comparison to his protective posture: crouched with his body bent over his knees, his arms crossed over his head. Even though he had never experienced an explosion before, some part of him knew to be afraid when I did not.

He looked up, and said as if explaining to himself, "I have never heard a bomb before!"

The most senior bomb technician extended his hand to help the man stand up, both of them smiling. We were all laughing, not harshly, but with the goal of making the man feel less embarrassed. The senior technician, holding the man's shoulder in a gesture of comfort, said, "Bombs are scary! I do not know why we're not all on the ground with you!"

Even as we laughed, the field manager and the rest of her team listened for any ancillary, accidental explosions (for example, due to a misfire). There was an anxiety to their attention that quickly reasserted the silence: everyone, even the office worker, now stood still and hushed facing in the direction of the demolition. In the shade of the pepper tree we were all waiting with our ears. Even the birds were waiting, or deafened. After several moments of focused silence, the senior technician said in a soft voice, "Beautiful!"

The Blast Radius

The blast radius extends out from the center of the explosion (in Lao, literally the bomb point, *jut laberd*) and describes the area that will be impacted by the blast. In her preparations for the demolition in rural Salavan Province described above, the field manager calculated the blast radius and safe points by taking into account the ordnance being demolished, the type of explosive being used, and the features of the area (such as soil composition, trees, and termite mounds). The blast radius was calculated with a spreadsheet, mapped to the meter, and marked on the ground by stakes and rope. After she precisely calculated the radius, the field manager sent technicians with bullhorns into the projected blast zone, instructing them to start at the bomb point and walk outward along its radii in order to clear out domestic animals and any wandering humans (see figure 3.1). She selected a safe point on the border of the impact zone, protected by the bulk of a large pepper tree, but still near enough to directly perceive the blast as sound. In clearance zones, hearing is an important tool for analyzing explosions that, due to the danger, should be observed at a distance. An explosion in a rural or forested area may only be visible at short distances but may be heard, with decreasing detail, for miles.

Sound is evidence of an explosion and, at near distances, is also a destructive force. When a bomb explodes, listening is something that happens to your whole body; sound is one valence of a destructive power that is passing through you and that can be physically painful in and of itself. The detonation of explosive ordnance produces a supersonic blast wave of pressurized air that, at its slowing fringe, degenerates into audible sound. Near the center of the detonation, the blast wave is too fast and irregular to be heard. At or near the bomb point, this sonic energy is experienced as physical force; visceral, destructive, deadly. These blast waves, characterized by massive changes in pressure, move through the body and produce resonant trauma such as deafness, nosebleeds, concussion, nausea, and inhibited respiration. Blast waves may propel fragments, which the design of some bombs amplifies via embedded shrapnel or fragmentation. Blast waves may throw victims against stationary objects. Smoke and heat spread by these waves may cause further injuries. In contrast to experiences of hearing on the margin of the blast radius, an explosion is commonly physically deafening at closer range. Hearing an explosion is only possible for able listeners at the fringes of the expanding blast where the pressure wave has degenerated into

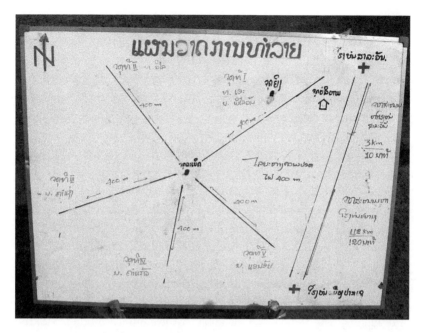

FIGURE 3.1 A plan for a controlled demolition showing the blast radius and safe
points as five radial lines. The central dot is the detonation point, the center of
the blast. The plan also shows the location of and distance to the
nearest hospitals. Photo by the author.

safely audible sound but has not yet collapsed into silence. Listening occurs
in a shifting concentric zone surrounding an explosion; a zone between silence (at the margins) and death (at the bomb point). A comfortably audible
sound at four hundred meters may be deafening at ten meters and deadly
silent at one. Violence, sound, and silence are intimately related experiences
for people inhabiting military waste–contaminated areas.

Throughout this chapter, I use the term "apprehension" to counter
possible sonocentrism, by which I mean the cultural practice of centering
able-bodied listeners and the audible to the exclusion of other forms of perception. Apprehension conveys the paired practice of perceiving an explosion and fearing it. Listening is only one valence of possible apprehension.
This explosive form of sonic violence cannot be reduced to its acoustics; nor
is the experience of being on the audible fringe of a blast radius limited to
people with good hearing. Apprehension marks the threshold of a fearful
awareness; a movement into a space of latent violence wherein one's home

may be on top of a cluster munition strike. Apprehension describes one's awareness of this parallelism of military wasting and everyday living. Sound and listening, as a practice that marks one's position in relation to the explosion, is a key means of inculcating this awareness. My use of "apprehension" refutes a "simple hearing/non-hearing binary" in the study of sound and invites further analysis of extra-auditory experiences of sound (Helmreich 2016, 167). I develop apprehension via a kind of unsound ethnography; an ethnography carried out by listening at the margins of a sound that people do not want to hear but listen for, nonetheless. Steve Goodman (2012, 198) theorizes "unsounds" as sonic phenomena at the "fuzzy periphery of auditory perception, where sound is inaudible but still produces neuroaffects or physiological resonances" that may be felt as ambient affective states, tactile vibrations, organ resonances, or physical trauma. Unsounds are *un-* in the sense of *un*conscious (a deeper process enfolded within consciousness) rather than in the sense of *un*comfortable (the opposite of comfort). At perilously near distances, the sound of the explosion refutes itself, is deafening or deadening. The audible and inaudible dissolve into each other, with the explosion's vibrational effects rupturing simple binaries between hearing/nonhearing or listening/deaf.* Explosions produce a social space for listeners and deaf alike; at the same time, listening and deafness are more likely possibilities at different distances from the bomb point. For my interlocutors in military waste–contaminated areas, the sound of an explosion also indicates the presence of other bombs nearby, yet to explode. This expectancy of future violence is also part of my theorization of apprehension as a crucial unsound affect. Pervasive military waste contamination, due to the extreme and latent danger, provokes transformations in sensory, affectual, and embodied experiences in space and time. The technical attunement of a bomb technician's senses and skills in order to perceive an explosion from afar is one example of the embodied experience of apprehending blasts and inhabiting hazardous areas. This chapter examines the apprehensive embodiments occurring on the edge of the blast radius, in the concentric zone where perception and survival are likely. As both a theorist and a fieldworker

---

* I use "deaf," lowercase, to encompass experiences of being temporarily deafened or permanently deafened by a blast. This is in distinction to "Deaf," capitalized, which conventionally refers to cultural communities of the deaf, commonly bounded by sign language use (Mills 2015).

learning to apprehend bomb blasts, sound is my entrance into this complex domain of embodiment and endangerment.

I front this chapter with two quotes: one by Nancy on the extremities of listening, and one by Frank on the difficulty of describing bomb explosions. Is Frank correct that the sound of a bomb is only the sound of the word itself—until one has felt it explode? Rather than escaping this quandary by retreating into abstract theory, I choose to focus on the gut-wrenching expectancy of an explosion, the apprehension of a bomb going off. The task is sustained by its failures: the gap between hearing the word "bomb" and feeling a bomb is central to my fieldwork, my analysis, and my writing. This chapter is my effort to bring the reader to the edge of the blast where listening, reading, and academic analysis are possible and comparatively safe. Audible sound, Nancy wrote, is "precisely nothing else than its edge, this fringe, this margin." If audition only occurs on the fringes, what lies at the center of these sonic phenomena? What might the analysis of the blast radius contribute to our understanding of human audition and unsound affects? For readers unfamiliar with listening to war, the opening description of a controlled demolition is an invitation to listen at the fringe of an explosion—as Nancy says, "to be on the edge of meaning." My description of this demolition functions as a safe introduction to bomb blasts: no one was injured; the explosion was not an accident; and all involved had proper training, safety equipment, insurance, and medical support. Other explosions in this chapter will be harder to imagine: the sound of accidentally setting a bomb off with one's shovel, and losing an arm in the resulting blast. "A sound's salience and emotional charge depends upon the life histories of the people who hear it, and upon the comparative backdrop against which they listen to the sounds that are emplaced in a particular time and location" (Daughtry 2015, 38). Conveying the acoustic context compels very careful thought and respect toward my interlocutors and further listeners or readers. This requires careful attention to the phenomena that emplace a sound, where description functions as a form of acoustic evocation. A controlled demolition is one such context, the details of which may function to emplace the sounds for technicians and residents inhabiting a clearance site—and for you, as a reader whose senses may not be attuned to the sounds of war.

As a researcher studying these sounds, I also inhabit the margins of these explosions. What are the methodological and ethical implications of inhabiting this shared zone of sonic violence? To listen safely on the fringe of violent explosions, as I do in the demolition I described in the opening vignette? Explosions have an auditory pull (both repulsive and fascinating) that moves us into their radius whether or not we want to be pulled. Rather than resisting that pull, in this chapter, I deploy it to bring my readers within the margins of the blast radius. By reading this chapter, you are stepping further into this zone of attention toward war and military waste. In academia, we often already occupy positions of apprehending on the margins of blast zones. War, violence, and trauma are recognized and valued topics of study in anthropology. Much of this writing focuses on the ethics of representing violence in scholarship—what I examine as the gap between the word "bomb" and feeling a bomb. In anthropological writing on violence, "how does one even determine the appropriate magnitude of one's representation . . . let alone presume the possibility of concordance among representations and the correspondence of one's representations with the represented" (Daniel 1996, 120)? In this chapter, I respond to these debates with an analysis of the spatial dynamics of knowledge production in hazardous areas. Whether we acknowledge it or not, I argue, as scholars we are all on the margins of violence listening at Nancy's "edge of meaning." This voyeuristic element is, in part, a result of the spatial dynamics of violence. Violence pulls us in, but it also forces us to recognize that there is only so far we are able or willing to go before we will be destroyed. This often subtle push/pull dynamic is actualized in the study of explosives and military wastes—in my field site, the blast radius and its safe edge are not metaphorical. The edge of the blast is where scholarship is possible; venture too far in and the bomb will destroy you and itself.

Bomb technicians carefully calculate areas of safety and danger, precisely marking the radius of a blast. Using different tools and expertise, with different expectations for safety and danger, I can draw that radius differently. What is the safe range for ethnographic research? What is the proper distance for critiquing violence? Or for recognizing complicity in imperial systems of warfare? By intentionally expanding the blast radius to include my academic audience, I am calling attention to this common scholarly mode of creating meaning at the margins of violence. When I conducted research in confirmed hazardous areas, access to my chosen research topic directly increased my personal endangerment. This is not to claim that more danger, or more intimacy with violence, is desirable in ethnographic fieldwork. On the contrary, learning to position myself safely in confirmed hazardous areas (by walking marked paths, for example) was literally vital to my research. Rather, my claim is that this mode of ethnographic attention to violence has implications for anthropological knowledge production: it matters where we draw the edges.

As I discuss in greater detail in later sections, military waste and explosives clearance spatializes social roles in relation to the bomb point and radius. My position, as a researcher of military waste, was almost always behind something or someone: those that walked in front of me were guiding me down safe paths and shielding me from the brunt of a possible explosion. Danger shaped my field site, but I would not describe danger as a limiting factor in my ethnographic research (see chapter 1 for an extended discussion of hazards in fieldwork). Danger added another dimension to ethnographic data and often worked to further intimacy with my interlocutors. Danger produced a shared social field of possible action, a field that became a topic of study in and of itself: the blast radius. Inhabiting danger structured other social roles in my field site. For example, the office worker who had never heard a bomb explode before occupied a very different role in the blast radius from that of the field manager in charge of the demolition. Despite the fact that he worked for a clearance operator, his position was more analogous to my own in that both of us were entering this contaminated field and learning to apprehend explosions. In this way, the blast radius was a social field that I used to map social roles in relation to explosions.

I examine the blast radius as it is viscerally experienced; as a social and cultural phenomenon of haunting possibility and violent repercussions. I use the phrase "blast radius" to mark that I am transforming a technical term (describing a specific explosion) into a social-theoretical term (describing the sociocultural impact of explosive military waste). Sound is my chosen means of analyzing explosions safely at a distance. I approach the topic of war in this seemingly oblique manner quite pragmatically, as a participant auditor: Rather than trying to accurately speak for interlocutors (residents as well as bomb technicians), I focus on our shared experience of apprehending explosions. As I discuss in the following sections, my learned aptitude for apprehending is data on the experience of inhabiting danger in Laos. Drawing on my ethnographic data on the affectual, embodied, and sensed experience of being in the blast radius or on its edge in Laos, I examine several interrelating qualities of explosions: first, as a destructive phenomenon that one inhabits and apprehends, often as an auditory event. Listening becomes a safety skill and also sensory evidence of survival (to hear the blast is to survive it). Living in the blast radius is to inhabit disability and engage one's senses and one's body in the apprehension of physical danger. Finally, I analyze explosions as an event that can be experienced in terms of a Buddhist ontology of plangent, resonant, and suffering bodies. Note that not all sounds relating to bombs are explosions: in my explication of this resonant embodiment, I contrast Buddhist spoken tone poems with the sound of a bomb going off. This attention to nonviolent sounds in parallel with violent sounds extends my argument for parallelism in the study of war's aftereffects. Throughout this chapter, I examine my own presence on the edge of the blast radius as an incitement to consciously develop practices for researching and writing about violence.

Interlude: To the Bomb Point

After waiting and listening for the radio signal that the team had checked the demolition site for live ordnance, the remaining technicians and I entered the blast zone. We walked single file backward along the radii to the bomb point. As a safety measure in case an explosive item had been thrown from the pit without detonating, I was not permitted to walk in front of the line—though I knew the way. The songs of birds and the rustling wind had quickly reasserted themselves. Nearing the center, our path was scattered with many fists of broken earth pressing the grasses in places. This scattering of clods of earth increased until we stood at the rim of the pit itself: a crater about three meters across of loose earth, black rocks, chunks of sparkling metal, splintered roots, and broken trees oozing sap. The heat of the explosion was still in the bottom of the pit, smoking and shimmering in serpentine coils. To the side, a large tree had been snapped in half, the trunk pale blond, its bark shorn off completely like a pelt. Some recognizable pieces of bomb still remained—a sliver of a grenade's fin, a crescent-shaped chunk from the end of a rocket. The explosion had polished the rust off of the remaining metal pieces; they were bright iron gray and silver in places, like new. One of the technicians encouraged me to pick up a chunk of gray, shimmering metal that had been thrown nearly out of the crater.

"It is still hot," he warned me. And another said, "Don't take it!" But I did.

I nearly dropped it—it still throbbed with its own destruction. It felt like black tarmac on a hot day—both absorbing and radiating heat. I held it for a moment, soaking in the feeling, before dropping it back into the pit. These relics of a secret war destroy themselves and leave no evidence but traces.

Apprehension

Bomb explosions are rare in Laos, yet locals recognize the sound when it is heard. Audible over vast distances, explosions are primarily acoustic phenomena for most people living in military waste zones. In rural communities without easy or regular electricity, or access to major traffic corridors, bomb explosions have a unique sound that distinguishes them from the regular clatter of everyday life. Most of war-contaminated Laos is mountainous; the sound of a blast may reverberate among the mountains for miles. Collectively, these geographic, architectural, and socioeconomic features shape a "resonant acoustic territory" (Daughtry 2015, 201) for hearing the sounds of explosions. A young man living in Phonsavan recounted the first time he heard a bomb explode: "On Wednesday, we [are] supposed to do school work: we go collect firewood for the school. It is normal to go [to the] bush, forest. Finally, one of the boy[s], he just found [a] cluster bomb on his path and he throws it downhill and it explodes. The big noise! Adults [in the village] hear noise and ask who is using bombs, but nobody is."

This young man had handled bombs before but never experienced an explosion. Prior to the explosion, his father had taken him out into the forest to look for war scrap (his father was a war scrap trader, one of the adults that might be "using bombs" in his quote). In the forest, his father told him, "Be scared of *bombi*," and showed his son how to recognize various types of cluster bomblets (see figure 3.2). But knowing what a bomb looks like is far removed from really, viscerally understanding the danger implied by the innocuous metal objects in the forest. The boy and his friends had found many bombs in the forest before and thrown them back and forth like toys. This was the first time that a bomb had exploded during their play, and the first time that he had seen someone die from an explosion. He experienced an explosion firsthand and thereby came to understand the threat of physical trauma and death. At the same time, his ability to perceive the explosion indexed his distance—measurable in meters—from the deadly center of the cluster bomblet's blast radius. "[After the

FIGURE 3.2 A cluster bomblet found by the author in a field outside Phonsavan. Photo by the author.

explosion] a boy runs back to the village and adults come. They get him [the victim] to hospital and he died in hospital. After that, I stop going to the jungle almost three months. . . . I realized this [bomb] was dangerous after I saw an accident. . . . I learned that from explosion you could die or could be handicap."

There is a certain quality, or intensity, of experience that can only be understood when bombs explode. Across the handful of meters between himself and his friend, throwing the cluster bomblet between them like a toy, this young man learned the difference between hearing the word "bomb" and feeling an explosion. As I discussed in the introductory section, I employ the term "apprehension" to describe the fearful sensibility made possible by direct experiences of explosions. I activate the dual meanings of apprehension: first, as perceiving or understanding something; and second, as fearing that something terrible will happen in the future. The term describes a sensuous means of understanding rooted in the immediate, visceral fear of physical injury, disability, or death for oneself or others. Learning to apprehend explosions involves an existential affect of anticipation, expectancy, and inevitability about a future contaminated with military waste.

Apprehension delimits the sociocultural blast radius. If you can apprehend the explosion, you are in its radius. This is not to say that apprehension is a purely natural result of experiencing explosions. My claim is, rather, that learning to apprehend explosions is a sociocultural and natural-cultural process (Haraway 2003) provoked by local ontologies of danger and massive military waste contamination. These explosions have continued, with slowing regularity, for decades. The specific cultural features of this embodied affect are taught even to very young children. At a mine risk education training I attended, the instructor was faced with the difficult task of teaching children as young as five about their own mortality in relation to military waste. When I observed her class, the climax of the lesson involved her walking through the classroom with a grisly photo of a recent explosion in the province that resulted in the deaths of two children. In the photo, two small bodies sprawl in the umber leaves and grasses; one of the bodies has been split apart, pale pink organs spilling out in an unidentifiable mass that occludes the entire upper body of the child; the other child is lying loosely, his limbs weirdly twisted. In the background, a group of adult men stand without clear purpose. From the teacher's desk at the front of the class, I took a photo of this grisly visual aid (see figure 3.3). In my photo, the visual tension between the foregrounded children's corpses, with one shoe still on, and the backgrounded living children's feet, in bright lime-green galoshes, is poignantly evocative of what is at stake in these risk trainings. My photograph is already partially effaced—none of the children's faces are visible—which I present as a visual invitation through which readers may wrestle with their own sense of dislocated loss.

The mine risk education instructor carried this photo around the classroom, pointing at the corpses, looking each student in the eyes and asking, "Can they play? Can they sing? Can they eat? Can they dance?" The students answered, wide-eyed, "No. No. No. No." These students already had a working knowledge of what bombs look like—they had seen them in their village—but they didn't yet understand what happens at the center of a blast. This instructor's challenge was to impart an apprehension to children who have not directly experienced an explosion, and hopefully, as a result of her training, never will.

FIGURE 3.3 Teaching aids used in mine risk education training in
Savannakhet Province. The topmost photo is of a recent explosion in the province
that resulted in the deaths of two children. Photo by the author.

Hearing the blast is a vital component of this new apprehension. Listening for blasts is a way to apprehend explosions from the margins, without being in direct danger. In accounts of explosions, the experience often
starts with the sound of the bomb going off ("The big noise!"). An account
from another explosion: "I hear a really big boom, and we think, 'Oh, that is
them!' and all three are just gone! With the big bomb, all that is left to find
is an arm. We don't know who it is, but we bury it in the jungle."

As I recounted in chapter 2, this woman heard this blast in a truck on her
way to work at a mine. Her brother had previously died in a bomb explosion
when the two of them were children. Several decades later, she was still listening for the sound of explosions. She had known, through local gossip, that
a group of three war scrap traders had traveled into the jungle to dismantle a
large bomb they had found on a previous scouting mission. Using the sound
of the explosion (its qualities, direction, and intensity) as her guide, she was
able to predict that the scrap traders' expedition had ended in tragedy. As the
wife of the village chief, listening for explosions was a component of her and

her husband's duties to record explosions in the village and refer survivors to state- or humanitarian-run support services. In the sociocultural blast radius, the listening villagers and the victims together demarcate a shared area of endangerment with regard to explosive ordnance.

The sonic qualities of the blast radius are defined, at one extreme, by inattention or ignorance and, at the other extreme, by deafness or deadness. In the middle is a zone of apprehensive attention and potential danger. If there is no clearance operator currently clearing an area, the sound may indicate that a bomb has exploded and injured a member of the local community. People listen for the sound knowing that it may be their best alert that a family member has been involved in an explosion and may need medical care. In both of the examples in this section, the sound served to mark the explosion for the adults in the village, who were then able to come to rescue the victims. And in both cases, those caught nearest to the bomb point nevertheless died. "To witness war is, in large part, to hear it. And to survive it is, among other things, to have listened . . . *through* it" (Daughtry 2015, 33, emphasis in original). Victimhood, by contrast, is often marked by the inability to hear (due to hearing loss or death). Listening for violent sounds is a way to mark oneself as a survivor and locate oneself on the margin of a blast radius. Simultaneously, listening also indicates that one is occupying a contaminated zone composed of other explosive ordnance that has not yet exploded. In this contaminated zone, the apprehensive, listening subject is also a subject in possible danger.

Unsound Affects

For people inhabiting an area undergoing explosives clearance in Laos, the routinization of demolitions may further cause the sound of an explosion to be separated from the violence of war. For trained ears, the sound may become data on the success or failure of a demolition—the ontological parallel of a bombing. When systematically clearing a confirmed hazardous area, as in the ethnographic vignette that opens this chapter, teams may schedule daily or weekly demolitions of the items found during survey and clearance. There may be a period of time in the afternoon or early evening when explosions, due to regular controlled demolitions at the close of each shift, are expected. Explosions become a routine sonic element of this bomb ecology for both technicians and residents, creating a kind of sonic contamination. People listen to these repeated blasts to monitor the activity of teams working nearby. Technicians also listen to the sound of an individual explosion to gather information about the success or failure of a specific demolition. For example, in the opening vignette, the silence following a blast helped the senior technician to determine whether the demolition had been successful. These sounds territorialize contaminated areas. Technicians may develop a sonic map of the contamination and clearance work occurring in an area, as when a technician remarked, "Did you hear that? That was them demolishing an item on the other side of the village. The villagers get used to it. Between two and five PM every day all the operators are dem'ing [demolishing] their bombs and it is common to hear the explosions all around the valley."

I strained my ears to catch this fleeting auditory evidence, but never acquired the ability to identify explosions over great distances. Jonathan Sterne remarks that sound studies "begins with hearing the hearing of others" (2015, 74). I relied on my interlocutors to tell me when they heard nearby teams demolishing items. Each sound was identified by my interlocutors as evidence for controlled demolitions: the type of blast, the location of the blast, the time of day, and their knowledge of nearby teams in action contributed to this assessment. At no point in fieldwork did I knowingly hear or experience an accidental explosion. My inability to hear blasts from afar indicated to me that I was not equally enmeshed in this bomb ecology. I was in the blast radius, but not listening in the way that other people were listening. Listening for explosions is a social act, and the blast radius is a social space. I was moving into this space, cultivating my own apprehensive listening. The social, embodied dynamics of this space enabled my interlocutors to hear what I could not. I was listening as an ethnographer while my interlocutors in the clearance sector were listening as bomb technicians.

For many of my interlocutors, the sound itself marked a threshold of comprehension: whether I had heard an explosion indicated my intimacy with military waste, and therefore my ability to understand the content of our interviews. The sound acquired the parallel repulsion and fascination of a siren's song: I dreaded hearing an explosion due to its associations with death, while, simultaneously, I desired to hear it as a way to gain the recognition of my interlocutors and better understand their experiences. I wanted to hear it and did not want to hear it. These sounds also carry an intense, negative emotional charge for many of my interlocutors—they didn't want to hear them either, and yet listened for them. This was very unsound listening. These sounds and unsounds of war constitute another form of hazardous data that provoked me to adapt my ethnographic method (see chapter 1). Thankfully, I never heard an accidental explosion and thus never had to weigh my appetite for the sound against the threat it implied. Instead, I sought out ways to hear explosions without the threat of injury: controlled demolitions conducted during routine clearance. I made the choice not to audio record explosions. This was largely pragmatic since my inexpensive audio recorder was completely incapable of recording explosions with any accuracy (I had not gone into the field expecting to record explosions), and even the most faithful recording would have not captured the meanings and affects provoked by these sounds.

My choice not to incorporate recordings is an analytical choice not to focus on sound as the central quality of this phenomenon. Hearing is a vital, but ancillary, part of learning to apprehend bomb blasts. The sound, in and of itself, is inadequate for cultivating these powerfully fearful affects. The sound has synesthetic abilities, where awareness in one sense (hearing) conditions a mix of perceptions and fears. By not incorporating recordings into the presentation of my research, I am inviting my audiences to imagine their own apprehensive listening. This mimics my field experiences: in the first few months of fieldwork, before I had heard an explosion, I woke up afraid during an intense monsoon thunderstorm. I was half hearing the explosion in my dreams, dreaming that the sound of the thunder was a bomb going off. To appease myself, I got out of bed and looked outside: The rain had temporarily abated, but thunder still resounded across the dark city. The streets glistened slick black, empty even of the lights and sounds of women rising early to prepare food for the morning alms. No sign of alarm, no police, no rushing neighbors, no plume of smoke. Nothing looked out of place. Later, after taking my morning shower, I looked long at myself in the fogged bathroom mirror, tracing my reflection in the condensation.

FIELDPOEM 21

> There is another sound
> that I don't hear
> nothing makes it go off
> —breath on a mirror; the word faintly reappears

This poem exists in the space between hearing the word "bomb" and feeling an explosion. The mixed audiovisual metaphor conveys the disturbing synesthesia of words, sounds, and feelings that characterizes sonic violence. The poem is also evidence of my growing sensitization to my fieldwork topic: an apprehension of future sounds, future dangers.

Being at the Bomb Point

I opened this chapter with an image of a planned blast radius, created to facilitate an explosives demolition. Another version of a blast radius is illustrated by a mural at the UXO Survivor Information Centre in Phonsavan, the capital of Xieng Khouang Province. In the demolition described in the opening vignette, the explosion was controlled and purposeful. In this section, I turn to another type of blast radius: one that is unintentional and causes injury to the people caught in its impact zone. This type of blast is technically called an accident, a term that I include for its technical meaning and colloquial use, but generally eschew for its obfuscation of postwar violence as accidental (see my discussion of accidents in the introduction). The center assists victims and survivors of explosions by coordinating medical services between government and NGO providers and facilitating physical, social, and economic rehabilitation. The type of support is specific to each person, but might include transportation to a clinic, training in small business finance, or a loan for purchasing livestock. The center additionally acts as a hub for a local survivors' association and other advocacy activities. The center's exhibition space displays portraits of survivors accompanied by dismantled inert cluster submunitions that visitors may safely handle. The main wall of the exhibition space is dominated by a large mural of a bomb explosion and its aftermath (see figure 3.4).

WHAMM!! The explosion is symbolized by a central exclamation—a word that describes both a sound and a force. The shockwave is portrayed as a series of concentric sharp bursts, starkly drawn in black and white. Vibrating lines of percussion project out from the central exclamation. A twisted pair of glasses and a tool are visible at the edges of the blast, implying the invisible presence of a person at the center—also serving as metonyms for dismembered body parts. The near-anonymity of the person (wearing glasses, working with tools) at the center of the blast indicates a leveling of identity down to the experience of being blown up. Rippling outward in jagged repercussions, the bomb explodes through the unseen person's dreams, jobs, family, school, friends, and health (symbolized by words written in both English and Lao). The blast is represented simul-

FIGURE 3.4 Mural at the UXO Survivor Information Centre in Phonsavan, Xieng Khouang Province. Photo by the author.

taneously as a physical process (with shockwaves) and as a social process (changing social roles and abilities). It is as if the explosion has a lingering vibrational effect and continues to reverberate, far beyond the prescribed blast zone, as survivors are learning to use a prosthetic arm, negotiating their abilities at work, or trying to complete their education. The blast radius has features far more insidious and encompasses an area far greater than its zone of simple destruction. To be a victim or survivor of an explosion is, in part, to be transformed into the center of an ongoing blast whose radius is defined by the social and cultural impact of the explosion upon one's own life and community.

The difference between a demolition and an accident is partially a difference of position, and thus perception, within the blast radius. Where technicians at a demolition carefully cultivate their distance from the explosion, and thus mediate their perception of the blast, a person involved in an accident is likely to be at the bomb point itself. The two explosions may be technically similar, but the two blast radii have very different sociocultural limits and embodied consequences and affects. For a person caught at the center of the impact zone, the blast is deafening, literally an assault on the senses. Temporary deafness is common and may become a permanent impairment for survivors of explosions.* This form of deafening highlights the tension between the blast's acoustic impossibilities (it can't be perceived at near distances) and its intense affective and embodied effects. Ana María Ochoa Gautier asserts that in many cosmologies, "the presence or absence of sound . . . stands as the very mediator of the presence or absence of life" (2015, 189). At the moment of the explosion, caught at the very center of the blast radius, the victim has passed the threshold of sound, which is also the threshold of life itself. A person cannot safely enter the core of the explosion; the explosion destroys itself and anyone or anything at its core. The center's mural and the field manager's map represent the blast radius as experienced from the margin and seen from above. This is the point of view of a bomb technician or of a bomber, not of a victim. The victim at the center of the mural is obscured, sensed by the viewer only as lingering, ghostly traces: a pair of glasses, a farm tool. It can be difficult to identify what remains after the explosion has settled; victims' bodies may be completely destroyed or retained only as unidentifiable pieces. Point of view from the bomb point is destroyed. Instead, the point of view in the mural and the map is from the outside of the blast, looking in, listening, and waiting.

This view from the margins is pragmatic: perception and danger are inversely correlated as one nears the bomb point. At the center of the blast, human sensory abilities break down completely. A survivor recounted to me that he lost all perception at the moment of the explosion except for his sense of pain: "I feel pain throughout my whole body. I did not know what was missing." Deafened, blinded, and in shock, an entire day passed before he was able to perceive that he had lost his left arm. For his listening kin in the village, the sound of the cluster submunition exploding alerted them to the event, provided clues to the type of ordnance, indicated the location of the explosion within the village, and thus enabled them to quickly arrive on site

* According to the first national survey of victims of UXO explosions in Laos, roughly 4 percent of surveyed victims sustain permanent impairments to their hearing. This survey did not record temporary hearing impairments after the explosion. Also not included are hearing impairments to those caught in the blast radius but not identified as "victims" (a slippery term) by the enumerators. Injuries to the head, neck, ears, and eyes account for roughly 18 percent of all recorded permanent injuries. The survey only recorded sensory impairments in seeing and hearing (Boddington and Bountao 2007).

in order to transport him to the nearest hospital. He was immediately sent to surgery, where his maimed arm was amputated into a workable stump. He shortly recovered his sensory abilities, and, while his left arm was unrecoverable, ultimately he received a prosthetic arm from the government-run prosthetics factory. The bomb point is a blind spot in his life; he had no direct experience or memory of the explosion itself. The explosion produced a lapse in his memory, a moment out of time and impenetrable to his senses. In contrast, his family's experience of the explosion was profoundly shaped by their ability to hear and respond to the blast.

The spatial and temporal dynamics of being at the bomb point present unexpected challenges to scholarship. The possibility of hearing an explosion demarcates a zone of danger and apprehensive attention, while also delimiting a sensory blind spot, a central area that destroys itself. This central zone of confounding possibility is where the figure of the ghost, the undead or the nearly dead, resides. I have built my argument in this chapter upon apprehension, embodiment, and sound. This is partially a result of conducting fieldwork from the safe margins: my position within the blast radius shapes the kinds of data and analysis that are available to me. I find that as I write myself nearer the bomb point, these concepts and terms become inadequate. Apprehension loses all theoretical meaning when a bomb explodes in one's hands. Hearing is impossible when standing at the bomb point. The explosion destroys perception, including scholarly attention. Theory turns in upon itself such that the theoretical concepts that apply at the margins become convoluted and warped farther in.

Echoes

There are perceptual differences between a wartime explosion and a postwar explosion. For example, a rocket deployed during wartime produces the arching sound of falling to earth, slowing, catching speed until the sound cracks into a thin whine before finishing in the low boom of impact and detonation. Evocatively, J. Martin Daughtry (2015, 68–69) recounts an American service member's description of the sound of a rocket: "a ripping noise, where it sounded as though . . . they're kind of ripping through the sky" before detonating. By comparison, a rocket exploding in modern Laos is not preceded by the sound of falling or by any other auditory triggers of war such as the sounds of planes overhead, armored vehicles moving nearby, or recent gunfire. There is only the immediate low, earthy boom pushing up from the soil where the rocket has been buried, possibly for half a century. What, during the Vietnam-American War, was experienced as a cohesive auditory event is now split into several parts: the final boom occurs fifty years after the initial, swooping crack of the bomb falling from the sky. Even separated by decades (or potentially centuries; many bombs remain explosive for hundreds of years), I choose to refer to the second half of this phenomenon (the explosion) as violent rather than accidental. The final explosion is temporally linked to the Vietnam-American War bombings, even if the perpetrators of that bombing are no longer directly acting in Laos. The bomb has become its own agent, separate from the pilots who dropped the bombs, the artillery personnel who shot the rockets, or the soldiers who placed the land mines. At the same time, the present explosion exceeds the past bombing: the blast becomes something other than a bombing and is no longer a direct military act.

The contemporary detonation is an echo from a war that ended nearly fifty years ago. "An echo is nothing if not historical. To varying degrees, it is a faded facsimile of an original sound, a reflection of time passed" (Smith 2015, 55). Echoes are ghosts of sounds produced by latent or lapsed consequences. My explication of echoes builds upon my development of a hauntology of military waste (see chapter 2). The sonic phenomena under analysis are not reproductions or recordings of past sounds; these are the actual explosions, reverberating fifty years after the bomb was initially dropped. People are living in an acoustic territory of echoes: not only the latent blasts buried in the rice fields but also the echoes waiting to resonate in these mountain valleys. Bomb blasts are a refrain in the Deleuzian sense of a repeating sound that produces its territory (Deleuze and Guattari 1987). Sounds territorialize via the intermingling of bodily sensations, affects, physical vibrations, and cultural auditory practices. Explosions produce their own resonance, their own echoes, which have the effect of territorializing space and time through periodic repetition. The time or distance between blasts is constitutive, rather than disruptive, of this territorializing process. A simple mortar explosion may be analytically split into several overlapping sounds: the initial retort of the shell being fired from the barrel; the whine of the projectile flying in a high arc; the deep boom when it hits its target, which may or may not include its immediate explosion; ancillary sounds such as buildings collapsing; and, last, the echo of these sounds reverberating in the surroundings. In this simple example, each acoustic even may be separated in space and time from each other event. For example, there may be no audible echo, or rather a lapsed silence, until the sound wave hits something and reverberates back to listeners. The acoustics of military waste highlight the auditory qualities of sounds experienced by listeners only as individual events at each heterogeneous instance of interaction—not as a continuous event unfolding linearly. "[Sound] waves may travel, but sounds do not. They become present at reception" (Helmreich 2015, 228). From the position of listeners, the echo originates in a prior time and another location; a sound out of time and out of place.

As with haunting, the ghost of the sound doesn't need to be heard for the affect to manifest. These are phenomena that feed on the peripheries of perception. Failure to promptly manifest may, in fact, produce a more arresting apprehension than that produced by immediate experience. Explosive military waste is a form of "specular violence" (Mbembe 2013, 132) that pushes people to the margins of life. Target populations are purposefully confined to zones of recurring, ongoing danger—to "*death-worlds*, new and unique forms of social existence in which vast populations are subjected to conditions of life conferring upon them the status of *living dead*" (Mbembe 2003, 40, emphasis in original). A young man employed by the UXO Survivor's Centre in Phonsavan explains how an explosion continues to significantly impact his life six years later: bound to regular surgery in order to remove increasingly delicate shards of shrapnel from his body, he was forced to drop out of school and return to his family farm. He indicates the mural, saying, "These are the things that change after a UXO explosion. But people who are . . . disabled by UXO still want health, dreams, school." Turning to me with new urgency, he explains, "I am a UXO survivor. Before [the] accident, I went to school in Luang Prabang. My family is very poor, so I go back to help them. I go out to dig potatoes with a hoe. I hit something hard and hear a *thunk*. I think it is a stone. But it is a bomb and it explodes."

He walks me over to one of the center's displays of inert *bombies*. "One of these," he continues, handing a defused BLU-26 to me. It is painted brown, heavier than it looks even when emptied of explosives, large as two fists pressed together, with a spiral pattern expanding out from its two poles. The cases of BLU-26 cluster submunitions are saturated with tiny metal balls of shrapnel, intended to cause lingering damage to the bodies of victims when the item explodes. They are designed to disable, rather than merely kill. Pointing in turn to his arm, his legs, his chest, and his stomach, he explains that he can feel the pieces of metal in his body, their hardness under his skin, their changes in temperature with the weather. His surgery is ongoing, and he has been unable to finish his degree. He has been kept "alive but in a *state of injury*" (Mbembe 2003, 21, emphasis in original). This man is living inside the blast radius and has taken on "a form of death-in-life" experienced as regular, repeated injury (21). Being a survivor has also exposed him to significant stigma, restricting his already limited social prospects. As I describe in later sections, this stigma is rooted in common Lao Buddhist explanations of explosions, where a single bomb blast is indicative of ongoing karmic cycles of misfortune. His aborted education and career make sense within this local ontology as further karmic reverberations for bad actions in this or previous lives. Far beyond the merely physical blast radius of the BLU-26, the pieces of the bomb continue to move through his body, his career, his education, and his personal life six years after the detonation.

Inhabiting Disability

In military waste zones, the possibility of further destruction haunts people's experiences of explosions and interactions with victims. In the logic of this form of survival, one's own liveliness turns into apprehension that one's community is contaminated and future explosions are inevitable. I contend that in military waste zones, people come to inhabit disability as a zone of morbid or disabling possibility (Zani 2015). For many, being in danger becomes a disability in and of itself, regardless of whether one is physically injured in an explosion. The spatializing dynamics of the blast radius extend to the intimate spaces of the body. Military waste sets the possibilities for life and death in contaminated zones. The present section is an extension of my use of mortalism: ordnance has mortal agency, a deathly power that perpetuates itself via its own destruction (see my discussion of mortalism in the introduction). Here, I extend this insight to the analysis of apprehensive disability in military waste zones.

To inhabit disability is to live at risk, where endemic dangers become constitutive of daily life and embodied experience. Jasbir K. Puar, whose work I discussed in the introduction, refers to the imperial process of "disability to come" (2017, 107), whereby target populations are debilitated through widespread risks. "Rethinking disability through the precarity of populations not only acknowledges that there is more disability within disenfranchised and precarious populations, but also insists that debilitation is a tactical practice deployed in order to create and precaritize populations" (Puar 2017, 72–73). Puar calls for the "recognition that disability is already here" (2017, 90) in the daily experience of precarious living; with regard to my discussion of postwar haunting, disability is already here in the manner of a ghost that may or may not manifest, whose violent origin is already past. The latency of this form of violence is constitutive of its political efficacy. Like rotating a prism to diffract light, one's own physical ability and present safety are fragmented, replaced by an awareness of statistically likely injury latent in daily life. The surrounding ghosts may become visible under this harsh light— haunted by the specter of one's own mortality. This specular imperialism is one aspect of mortalism, the deathly power of explosive ordnance, but not its exclusive power. The blast radius is a social field inhabited by people with distinct lives and communities, beliefs, resources, and kinships—and not only a battlefield inhabited by soldiers.

Lindsay French (1994), who conducted fieldwork in refugee camps on the Thai-Cambodian border as the Khmer Rouge were collapsing, is one of the few anthropologists to analyze war-related disabilities in Southeast Asia. The guerrilla tactics that characterized the Vietnam-American War theater left a legacy of land mines along the border, deliberately set with just enough force to maim but not to kill. She describes lower-leg amputations as the war's "signature . . . indelibly inscribed on the bodies of the Cambodian people" (French 1994, 71). The primary response to the highly prevalent bodies of amputees was fear. This affective, apprehensive response was due not only to the increased social vulnerability of the disabled and their kin, nor only to the diffuse risks of living in war waste zones. French links this fear up to the Theravada Buddhist cosmology common in the region: disabled people were understood to manifest dangerous and disorderly powers. Survivors were often assumed to be possible sources of further violence and injury to others in their communities. Survivors' physical disabilities signaled a further "'karmic' handicap," meaning that their Buddhist merit and spiritual abilities were somehow degraded (84). Explosions were evidence of this spiritual disability, predating but also precipitating physical disability. Victimhood was evidence of spiritual misfortunes playing out in this life, thereby signaling that victims and their communities were at greater risk of further misfortune.

The qualities of military waste contamination are multifarious and not at all restricted to direct physical effects. The spiritual effects of pervasive contamination and ongoing maiming are crucial to understanding people's debilitating experiences of apprehension. Forty years after French's fieldwork, Tine M. Gammeltoft (2014) examined people's fear of war-related disabilities as a sociopolitical force that continues to haunt contemporary Vietnam. This "spectre of disability," the fear of war-related disablement, is imagined by many as an unpredictable, unruly obstacle to personal prosperity or national development (Gammeltoft 2014, 154). The latency of Agent Orange contamination in particular (its invisible risks and multigenerational effects) only heightens the sense of a prosperous future deferred by war-related disabilities. "Spectre," here, is not a metaphor. In Laos, bomb explosions are often colloquially understood to be set off by angry ghosts (*phi dtai hong*), with the ghosts themselves generally having been past victims of the war and its wastes (see my discussion of the ghost mine in chapter 2). Due to the destructive nature of explosions, it is often impossible to obtain, and thus to properly memorialize, the complete corpse of the deceased victim. The absence of a proper funeral ritual nearly guarantees that the deceased will become an angry ghost. Angry ghosts are extremely dangerous and may enact vengeance for their bad death by perpetuating similar tragedies upon their kin and others related to them in life. The site of an explosion may become haunted by the ghost of the victim, who in turn may trigger further deadly explosions.

Apprehension is partially a process of "ethical attunement" that draws on religious explanations of endangerment and violence (Hirschkind 2015, 167). Listening is a vital component of this ethical attunement: "Religious traditions have distinct repertoires of natural and unnatural sounds that signal the presence or activity of spiritual or otherworldly forces" (Hirschkind 2015, 170). The sound of each explosion may be heard as evidence of a cycle of violence unfolding over time, connected to other explosions, injuries, and deaths in the village. These sounds have a religious agency that acts upon the listener in order to "attune human perceptual faculties and expressive repertoires in accordance with a society's place in a divinely ordered universe" (169). In profound contrast to Hirschkind's discussion of the trumpets of angels, bomb blasts are not "divine acoustics" announcing the gate of heaven. Rather, each blast contributes to an apprehensive sense of one's own mortality and karmic possibilities, while further signaling the possible presence nearby of an angry ghost. The sound of explosions punctuates everyday life with another temporality, one expressing ongoing cycles of war, violence, and haunting.

As I noted earlier, Heonik Kwon (2008) and Mai Lan Gustafsson (2009), examining the haunting of postwar Vietnam, demonstrate that spiritual relations may manifest in the bodies of the living as violent possessions, illness, bad luck, and death. The possessed often experience injuries that repeat the injury that caused the initial victim's death: in this logic, fathers and sons may both lose their hands in separate, but spiritually linked, explosions. The family of the victim is at higher risk of further misfortune—meaning that the blast radius extends outward and encompasses the kin of the victim regardless of whether family members were physically present within the blast zone. In this way, the living become entangled in relations with the violently dead. Living in contaminated areas means to inhabit disability, via these spiritual relations of resonant embodiment, regardless of whether one is directly impacted by an explosion. Ongoing violence due to military waste explosions continually arrests people's abilities to correctly memorialize the dead and stave off further cyclical violence. Gustafsson describes the postwar period of the Vietnam-American War as "the age of wild ghosts" (2009, 70). In the present tense, the war is "infusing millions of fresh souls into the spirit world, and relegating millions more to a hellish status as wandering ghosts" (Gustafsson 2009, xiii).

Resonant Embodiment

In contrast to the unsound affects I have discussed in previous sections, monks use sounds to produce feelings of peace in listeners. This is another component of the spiritual relations of resonant embodiment that I introduced in the previous section. The sonic qualities of the blast radius include specific "religious sonorities" rooted in overlapping spirit cult and Theravada Buddhist concepts of danger (Hirschkind 2015, 166). My interlocutors often referred to those killed in explosions as victims of "unnatural death," a euphemism for the deceased that have become angry ghosts. It is unlucky to audibly reference these ghosts—even the sound of the word for "angry ghost" is unlucky—lest the speaker invite their sinister attention. Ghosts are listening. Speaking of ghosts or death directly has a resonant effect that ripples outward, potentially alerting other ghosts and setting off other unfortunate events. By contrast, people with great spiritual training (such as monks and other venerable persons), may safely discuss misfortunes and address ghosts directly in order to appease them and arrest these cycles of violence. In comparison to "karmically handicapped" victims, monks have the spiritual abilities to safely manage these disorderly, ghostly powers.

Not all sounds related to military waste are explosive or destructive. The sound of monks chanting a poem at a ritual for victims of explosions is contemplative and calming: waves of sonorous words, textured by a variety of pitched voices, punctuated by the scratch or hiss of consonants and layered with the breathy inhalations of individual monks. I introduced some of these sonorous effects within my discussion of Lao poetic parallelism in chapter 1. At the Buddhist-based mine risk education training that I attended at the Peace Temple in Phonsavan, monks were reciting poems that they had written themselves or as a group. The poems use the format and language of Buddhist tone poems to address issues related to military waste, victimhood, and disability. In these poems, there is a conscious engagement with risky words describing ghosts, death, bombs, and victimhood. Monk-poets also make extensive use of words in Pali or Sanskrit that are beyond the comprehension of most listeners and some speakers (many novices and monks are not fluent in the Pali texts that they recite from memory). Trying to engage with these risky and sacred words as ethnographic evidence proved frustrating; I slowly realized that in seeking translations or commentary, I was asking my interlocutors to engage with the poems in a foreign manner. Additionally, as a woman, I was positioned as a listener, an audience member, in my interactions with monk-poets. Becoming an ethnographer of these poems involved learning to put down my field notebook, letting go of recording or understanding what I was hearing, and listening attentively.

The sound of a poem—the play of vowels, consonants, words, and tones—is crucial to its efficacy. It is important that a poem sound "soft" and "smooth" (*kham fang feuy*, good words smoothing it out) so that it is easy to listen to. Discussing smoothness, a Lao poet explained to me, "It is like music. It is easy to memorize and you can practice singing it." Listeners should be able to feel the poem, and be affected by the poem, without understanding the words. Some of my monk interlocutors emphasized that understanding the words might actually detract from the poem's peaceful affect: "You have to listen to the song of peace in the poem—if you want the meaning, you have to get it from the normal sentence." The sound-feeling of smoothness is an acoustic palliative for all beings, living or dead. These smooth sounds resonate within and between entities, across the boundaries of this world and the afterlife. One monk-poet explains to me, "The poems are good for the deceased [ghosts]. We give loving-kindness for those dead from war, for families of those who pass away. We make them calm and have deep full understanding [of the dharma]." Due to their spiritual abilities, monks are able to directly address and mitigate the ghostly dangers of military waste. Monks use the power of sacred, spoken words to smooth and soften bodies and spaces contaminated by military waste.

Peaceful poems and violent explosions, understood in parallel, contribute to my analysis of resonant embodiment. I use the word "resonant" to imply mutuality and parallelism, against simple binaries of subject/object, object/ground, self/other, or living/dead (Erlmann 2014). The resonant qualities of sound itself imply and invite this form of analysis: "Sound waves transfer between media (air, water, solids), and can be experienced by sensory domains beyond the ear. Vibrations, visual recordings, and speech gestures are all possible components of an acoustic event. The ear itself is a composite organ which hears by mechanical and electrical means" (Mills 2015, 52). While often experienced as an auditory phenomenon, these boundary-crossing qualities of sound exceed the realm of strictly human acoustics—resonance becomes its own phenomenon. Resonant embodiment refers to the spectrum of vibratory, embodied effects occurring within the blast radius: not only resonant traumas caused by sonic pressure waves (such as impaired hearing), but also other sonorous and auditory processes such as learning to listen for explosions in one's village and (in this section) Buddhist tone poems designed to produce peaceful affects in victims and their kin. As these poems imply, explosions are part of the sensory and affective attunement of religious persons, signaling roles and duties within the blast radius. Monks and laity develop their moral discernment and proper affectivity by listening and letting these sounds affect them; as a way of ethically responding to explosions within their village to care for victims or as a way of learning to cultivate internal peace after an explosion. Charles Hirschkind, speaking to the sonorous qualities of religious experience, remarks that "an art of listening mediates one's relations to a practical and moral world. . . . More than serving as a vehicle for symbolic content, sound and aurality are part of the material-sensory world that human life must accommodate and respond to in the course of constructing a valued form of life" (2015, 168). Explosions constitute clear injunctions to constructing valued forms of life.

In contemporary Theravada Buddhist practice, listening and chanting are valued ways to produce "body-awareness" as part of cultivating equanimity toward one's own sense desires (Collins 1997, 196). In Buddhist cosmology, moral progress necessarily manifests different kinds of bodies and worlds through time. More specifically, "the corporeality of the world, its inhabitants, and its temporal cycles are tied to the moral behavior of human beings" (Hansen 2007, 22). Attention to one's own body, and the bodies of others, is a way of attending to the moral corporeality of the world. Helping those that are suffering to feel at peace is one way to intervene into this moral-corporeal nexus; peace is a moral quality in and of itself, and also the corporeal ground for health and healing. Conversely, widespread maiming and endangerment is evidence of immorality and spiritual ruin. Monks contribute to Laos's postwar revival via intervention at the level of this moral-corporeal nexus, at the level of embodied affects. Peace, understood in this way, is detached from specific conflicts and becomes, rather, a state of spiritual ability, receptivity, and equanimity between and within beings. Benedict Anderson describes smoothness as an onto-ethical quality of power in the Southeast Asian region: "Smoothness [is] the quality of not being disturbed, spotted, uneven, or discolored. Smoothness of spirit means self-control, smoothness of appearance means beauty and elegance, smoothness of behavior means politeness and sensitivity" (1990, 50). The sonorous process of "smoothing" is also an ethical process that produces an embodied affect of peacefulness within and between beings.

Sacred poetry and military wastes, smoothness and unsound affects, all work within the same resonant field of force. In the Southeast Asian region, religions provide the primary conceptualizations of power (and disability, danger, and healing). As Shelly Errington describes in her work on contemporary Indonesia, regional cosmologies describe power as a field that people inhabit: "[Power is] a field of energy. The energy exists everywhere in the field but is unevenly distributed: in some places it is quite thin; in others, densely concentrated. The energy is continuous—there are no boundaries and no empty spaces, but only thinner and thicker concentrations. The energy in this field is distributed not only unevenly, but unstably. It is constantly moving, waxing and waning from particular locations" (1989, 58).

Power is an invisible field that condenses in particular entities and is generally characterized by the relations between entities. Power is a force that is always moving, and may be drawn from one center into the ambit of another. Understood at a distance, power may be represented as a field of pulsating centers with various gravitational forces. Anderson famously described power in Java as "a cone of light cast downward by a reflector lamp" (1990, 36). In other examples from this key article, he equates power to "the image of the burning-glass or the laser beam, where an extraordinary concentration of light creates an extraordinary outpouring of heat" (24). In Anderson's account, at the center of these radial fields of power there is always a human or humanlike agent—a king or other charismatic entity. The radial fields I am analyzing do not center on persons, but on bombs that enact their own vicious agency beyond the intentions of the human agents that initially deployed these weapons. An explosion may be understood as an expression of this power, the literal blast radius, that is produced even as the agent (the bomb) is destroyed. Bombs manifest a particular kind of nonhuman agency characterized by mortalism and deathliness (see my discussion of mortalism in the introduction). Building on canonical descriptions of power as distributed light or energy, I analyze explosions as literal examples of how power operates to produce the blast radius as a sociocultural field of apprehensive, deadly force.

My research demonstrates the sonorous qualities of this cosmology of power. Each bomb is "a center from which Power radiates," and sound is one of the indexes that one has entered its field of force (Anderson 1990, 74). Sound is one way that people perceive and manipulate these explosive powers. The affective power of the spoken word to produce internal states of peace enables survivors to stabilize their bodies and cultivate their spiritual abilities—to make their bodies resonant with these flows of power. Generating a state of internal peace is a necessary prerequisite for overcoming disability's karmic handicap. The poems also have a calming effect on listeners who are not direct victims; in this way, peace-generating poetry is understood to counter people's tendency to fear the disabled and those impacted by war.

Conclusion

Explosions are a form of "sonic warfare" that produces a fearful zone of potential danger and disability (Goodman 2012). This blast radius of sociocultural affects, which I have explored as forms of apprehension, are produced in addition to an explosion's destructive effects. The sociocultural blast radius is much larger than the immediate area of physical destruction. The sonic qualities of the blast radius, as I have theorized them, include the listening expertise of clearance technicians, the listening expertise of villagers living in contaminated areas, the unsound affects of apprehending violence and hearing echoes from past wars, the experience of inhabiting disability, and forms of resonant embodiment and dissonant violence. In each of these examples, the explosion emplaces those caught within its radius. Sound is my chosen way to delineate the features of this zone, while also demonstrating its multifarious effects. Yet sound, if limited to the merely audible, is profoundly inadequate to understanding these phenomena. Apprehending explosive military waste unsettles the boundaries between hearing and deafness, listener and sound, between beings and things, and between the living and the dead. Military waste, not least when animated by a vengeful ghost, demonstrates the "agentive acoustic dimensions of nonhuman entities in the affairs of humans" (Ochoa Gautier 2015, 189). At the center of the blast radius is a bomb, not a human. Even as the living human is decentered, human bodies are always features of these blast zones. Cluster bomblets and other explosive ordnance are designed to maim and kill humans. The blast radius embeds this threat to human life, even for those who inhabit its safe margins, and even in a controlled demolition where no one is injured. Being on the edge and being at the center of a blast are vitally, viscerally different— and both are unified by a shared concern for human mortality.

This research has necessitated an expansion of sound to include unsounds, resonances, and other vibratory phenomena beyond the merely audible. This was partially in response to the pragmatic dynamics of conducting fieldwork in confirmed hazardous areas. Listening at the margins of explosions became my primary position in the field, while also marking clear boundaries I could not cross. Listening was a limit-making and border-marking practice. My repeated failure to hear the sounds of explosions from afar, even as my interlocutors heard them, was one example of how sounds marked the limits of my abilities in this field site. Other ethnographic elements in the field (ones not directly related to sound) began to acquire sonorous qualities. In this way, I was becoming a participant auditor or a participant listener (Forsey 2010) as much as a participant observer. My expansion of sound to include unsounds is also a response to the ableist assumption within sound studies of a normally hearing subject. "Sound studies has a creeping normalism to it—that is, an epistemological and political bias toward an idealized, normal, nondisabled hearing subject" (Sterne 2015, 73). With regard to my experience of listening as a limit-making practice, Sterne advocates that sound studies scholars "hold onto the idea that the ways people can hear, the limits of that hearing, and the conditions of possibility for hearing all provide points of entry into what it means to be a person at a given time or place. . . . To study hearing is to study the making of subjects, which means it is also to study the denigration and unmaking of subjects" (2015, 73). Explosions are a particularly literal example of how sonorous phenomena can "unmake" people. People within the blast radius don't have to hear an explosion to be impacted by it. Deafness and silence are key to my engagement with sound studies.

Military waste may linger for decades or centuries in the places where war occurs—over time provoking new meanings and practices. In these zones, the temporal and territorial border between war and postwar, or battleground and village, breaks down. The two phenomena, war and postwar, are experienced in parallel. Cluster bombs and other explosive ordnance produce a spatiotemporal arrangement of power that territorializes and contaminates, especially subterranean spaces, social spaces, and spaces inside the body. The violence of the war is prolonged in the soil, such that living in these contaminated spaces becomes a form of war violence in and of itself. Living on the surface of these zones, life can be incredibly thin—humanitarian explosives clearance in Laos may only go as deep as twenty-five centimeters below the soil surface, the depth of a typical Lao plow. The potential for violence changes the nature of space, and therefore the qualities of social space. Achille Mbembe theorizes that air military power is an extension of colonial occupation into the air above, where bombers fly, and the ground below, where bombs linger, with the goal of "seizing, delimiting, and asserting control over a physical geographic area—of writing on the ground a new set of social and spatial practices" (2003, 25). The blast radius is an expression of these new social and spatiotemporal practices as shaped by people's apprehension of latent danger and disability. In the blast radius, the conditions of human existence bluntly manifest military action and political power decades after war officially ceases. These zones demonstrate how violence can be a powerful enactment of the political and social upon the very material of our lives.

FIELDPOEM 26
House Blessings

I walk into the dark
Sound of monks chanting next door
Turn on the kitchen light

Look out my open window—dark
Imagine seeing my window light up
Some other blessing

Conclusion

———

PHASEOUT

The Checkpoint

"That is where it happened."

My colleague pointed to a police checkpoint, a small square open-air structure with white half walls and a sloping green roof. The white walls were painted with ocher dust and tar from the road. The structure was elevated on a concrete base so that the police had a raised view of the four-way intersection. Two officers in green khaki uniforms sat on chairs within, staring out aimlessly, their hats off and resting on the wide railing. Their obvious boredom set them apart from the intersection bustling with cars, motorcycles, trash collectors pushing their handcarts, street vendors sizzling fresh rice snacks, and pedestrians. The traffic churned the air pale gold, suffused with the smells of gasoline, sizzling fat, and the fishy scum of the river that ran parallel to the road. Beyond the checkpoint grew a thin green lace of forest left uncultivated as a flood buffer between the road and the Mekong River. Only the upright black barrels of their twin AK-47s were visible leaning against the railing of the checkpoint, the guns identifiable by their height.

We were waiting on his motorcycle at a red light along one of Vientiane's major paved roads. Identical checkpoints were present at every intersection along this road, and at all the major intersections in the city. There was nothing outwardly remarkable about this one.

"Where what happened?" I asked.

He turned his head slightly behind, to speak to me in the pillion seat: "Where he disappeared. Sombath."

"Oh! To think, I drive past this checkpoint every day on my way to work."

"They just pulled him over and took him. Right there." He pointed again with his finger, definitively. His voice carried the sad notes of reminiscence, though he had to speak a little loudly over the din of the road. "I sometimes feel that he hasn't left. I think about him every time I drive through this intersection. I mean, who knows? Maybe he will come back tomorrow."

"So, it feels to you like he never left?"

"Yeah, because we don't know. We will never know what actually happened."

My interlocutor pointed out the ghost, the site of a haunting. Roadside shrines to the ghosts of car accidents are common in Laos; but this was different, significant precisely because there was no sign, no shrine, no corpse even to mark that the man had disappeared. The regular features of the intersection, crystallized in the standardized white-placard checkpoint, suddenly acquired a powerful arresting force: "The oppressed past or the ghostly will shock us into recognizing its animating force" (Gordon 2008, 66). Thus, my interlocutor's finger pointed out the door to a parallel world, one that he could see very clearly, and which he was inviting me to observe with him. Avery Gordon, analyzing political disappearances in Argentina, describes how everyday life became porous, riddled with potential entrances and exits: "the door of the uncanny, the door of the fragment, the door of the shocking parallel" (2008, 66). To be haunted by the disappeared is to be receptive to "the moment in which an open door comes alive and stops us in our tracks, provoking a different kind of encounter and recognition" premised on repressed correspondences (66). Late in 2016, almost five years after the disappearance, the police replaced the old checkpoint with a new one at the same location—nearly identical, but with built-in glass windows instead of open-air sides. The physical location of the disappearance had been erased and replaced with another, identical checkpoint. My interlocutor's efforts to fix the disappearance in space ("That is where it happened") had been undermined, made ambiguous—this checkpoint, but not quite *this* one.

In this conclusion, I lay out the series of correspondences that culminated in the end of my fieldwork in Laos—I present these accounts as a

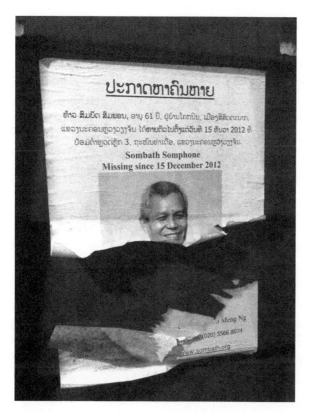

FIGURE C.1 Missing person posters for Sombath were put up, and just as quickly torn down, in Vientiane. Photo by the author.

prism for reflecting on the end of my book. These include the disappearance of Sombath, to which I turn in the next section; the shrinking of my research partnerships; and the phaseout of my primary research host. A series of recessions, retreats, and disappearances. It is one of the ironies of this research that I entered this field site expecting to contend with the dangers of explosions and found, instead, that I was more often contending with police harassment, espionage, censorship, and paranoia. As I have argued throughout this book, my experiences of police harassment and my experiences of military waste are both parts of a larger phenomenon of postwar remains/revivals. I have addressed these experiences collectively as hazards in an effort to eschew the overdetermining vocabulary of danger, risk, and (in this final conclusion) terror. The terror provoked by political disappearance both is ethnographically specific to Laos and indicates larger processes of postwar violence and state terror. My discussion of this specific form of violence forms the final component of my analysis of hazards and hazardous research methods. There is a parallel between the Secret War and these contemporary secret abductions—and the two together expand my analysis of postwar remains/revivals. The spectacular visibility of explosions, as discussed in chapter 3, are a counterpoint to disappearance. There is a bright contrast been the heightened data collection and analysis practices of bomb technicians and the erasure of knowledge that characterizes covert violence. I examine the implicit parallelism of disappearance as a final elaboration of my theory of parallel remains/revivals. The present analysis builds on my theorization of haunting as a component of authoritarian revival. Experiences of disappearance uniquely activate relations between presence and absence, war and peace, the living and the dead. I use these accounts of disappearance to examine the stakes in developing a hazardous research methods tool kit and to call for future research in former battlefields.

The Disappearance

A closed-circuit television (CCTV) camera, recently installed by the police in a new initiative to monitor antisocial behavior, recorded the disappearance in poor-quality video: On the evening of December 15, 2012, Sombath Somphone and his wife were driving their family jeep down a major Vientiane street. Crossing a large, four-way intersection, the jeep was pulled over at the police checkpoint. The jeep entered the zone of the CCTV camera, crossing into the circle of light from the street lamp next to the checkpoint. A blurry human figure exited the jeep, while other figures approached from the checkpoint. A black figure on a black motorcycle approached the checkpoint, dismounted, and got into the jeep on the driver's side; abandoning his motorcycle, the person in black drove the jeep away with Sombath's wife inside. The video footage has the quality of a dream in which objects and people are interchangeable. A white truck arrived and several figures, including presumably Sombath, got into the truck and were driven out of the view of the camera. The remaining figures returned to the checkpoint. His wife was driven home safely; Sombath never returned.

At the time of his disappearance, Sombath was sixty years old and had been carrying out development programs in rural Laos for more than three decades. He grew up as a rice farmer in Khammouane Province. As a young man, he received a scholarship to study in the United States, where he focused on education and agriculture. Returning to Laos in the early years of the revolution, he pioneered low-cost agricultural methods carried out via participatory development programs—efforts that he continued until he disappeared. He had recently retired from his position as director of a highly successful rural development training center that he had cofounded. He was known for his collaborative work on rural poverty reduction, farming, and public education—seemingly orthodox topics in a socialist regime. In 2005, in recognition of his achievements, he was awarded the prestigious Magsaysay Award for public service in Asia.

Rather than proving the disappearance, the CCTV video has remained persistently inscrutable. Shortly after the disappearance, in response to the family filing a report of a missing person, an officer at a local police station shared the CCTV footage with the family. The family recorded the footage on a personal digital device but was not provided with their own copy. This was the last time that the police cooperated in the investigation beyond the briefest public statements of ongoing interest. The persistent uncertainty of disappearance is confounding; but, taken together, the various rumors, videos, maps, case numbers, police reports, letters of concern, and testimonies shape their own ghostly accounting. There is an overwhelming sense that "a crucial aspect of what we need to know in order to understand disappearance is missing from the human rights reports and other documents" (Gordon 2008, 80). The sense of incompleteness and loss becomes constitutive of this form of data—evidence that one is encountering an absence. A key part of state-sponsored disappearance is the withholding or manipulation of proof such that, even when one has a video of the act itself, the disappearance remains unknowable and the missing unfound. This is an ontological intervention into the very experience of reality. The Lao state has refused outside assistance to decipher the fuzzy license plates or identify the model of the white truck. The original CCTV footage has not been released, though a bootlegged recording of that initial viewing at the police station was rapidly uploaded to YouTube and other video-sharing sites.

The modern practice of political disappearance is rooted in World War II Nazi programs of targeted, total erasure of populations and individuals (Rosenblatt 2015). The practice came to prominence again in a series of Cold War conflicts in South America in the 1970s and 1980s in which right-wing dictatorships targeted suspected political dissenters for secret abduction and execution (Rosenblatt 2015; Sluka 2000). The last quarter of the twentieth century saw a marked rise in forced disappearance, death squads, and other forms of extrajudicial, clandestine killings (Sluka 2000). In 1978, the UN General Assembly first recognized the practice of disappearance as a new and serious global concern. The rise of global "cultures of terror" (Taussig 1987) was linked to the Cold War American imperialist practice of supplying mixed military-humanitarian aid to proxy conflicts, including training in counterinsurgency methods such as disappearance. The CIA paramilitary operation in Laos (what I have referred to previously as the "Laos model") is a pioneering example of this type of proxy warfare. "Cultures of terror" refers to sociocultural systems in which "order . . . is maintained by the permanent, massive, and systematic use or threat of violence and intimidation by the state" against its own population, for whom "fear becomes a way of life" (Sluka 2000, 22–23). Michael T. Taussig, studying such systems as they emerged in South America, writes that state terror is experienced by target populations as "a death-space in the land of living [in which] torture is endemic" (1987, 4). These cultures of terror emerge on the local scale, articulating local and regional sociopolitical processes, while simultaneously being connected to international networks of militarism, imperial intervention, and humanitarian and human rights work. Individual acts of terror are part of much larger, global networks. It is clear that "classical authoritarian military dictatorships do not have a monopoly over state terrorism and state-condoned violence" (Warren 2000, 230). The Lao Party state draws on earlier forms of imperial and colonial control, including military-enforced curfews and armed checkpoints. There is a clear lineage of state terror that includes American paramilitary trainers introducing counterinsurgency methods into Laos during the Secret War.

There has been no effort to create a precise account of disappearances and other state violence in Laos, largely due to the fact that there was very little communication infrastructure outside of the capital city, no civil society or independent media, and closed borders for several decades, and retaliation was arbitrary and seemingly omnipresent. Among my interlocutors, disappearance was considered routine and unsurprising—this did not lessen the sense of threat and grief. Laos has largely managed to avoid scrutiny, focused on other authoritarian regimes, due to its enforced isolation and relative status with regard to its higher-profile neighbors (China, Thailand, Vietnam, Cambodia, Burma). When the Lao People's Revolutionary Party seized control in 1975, the new regime sent an unknown number (Evans [2004] speculates between ten thousand and fifteen thousand) to seminar or reeducation camps in the mountains, a euphemism for prison camps. None of these prisoners were ever charged legally. Many of them disappeared completely, their families left without even the certainty of death. The current Party state continues the practice of secret prison camps, and very little is known about these camps. The only instance of major political dissent, a students' prodemocracy rally in October 1999, was met with immediate retaliation. Five organizers for the rally were promptly arrested and sentenced in a closed trial to twenty years' imprisonment. Nothing has been heard about these "October protestors" since their sentencing eighteen years ago. Sombath's disappearance was the first high-profile case of disappearance in Laos to make it into the international mainstream media. In this way, Sombath's disappearance has come to stand in for every other instance of state-sponsored murder and abduction in Laos, even as the specific names of these other victims go largely unvoiced. The global response included statements of concern from the United Nations, the European Union, many humanitarian and human rights organizations, and several foreign governments including the United States.

The "fantasy space within which state violence operates" does not depend on objective evidence or actual threat (Aretxaga 2000, 46). It does not matter whether Sombath was or was not a subversive threat to the state. These fantasies of terror are efficacious by "binding actors to and in an alternate reality" in which the state has solidity, agency, and arbitrary power (Aretxaga 2000, 62). I nuance this claim by asserting that the "death-space" or "fantasy space" of state terror is not so much an alternate reality as an existing, parallel reality that moves alongside our own and threatens to open its doors to us, always. This binding happens for both state perpetrators of violence and civilian targets of violence; paramilitary forces, armed forces, insurgents, and civilian populations are all caught together via social ties and cultural affinities. The total effect is one of collectively skewing toward a parallel world of terror that becomes all the more powerful for its arbitrariness and ambiguity.

Haunting Development

A private online forum for the Lao development sector to which I subscribe has, for the last several years, organized digital events on each anniversary of Sombath's disappearance.* During one of these anniversary events, a forum

---

* This is a private forum, by invite only, considered a safe space to voice controversial opinions (up to a point) that do not fit within the official development discourse. Sombath was a prominent member of this group prior to his disappearance. I have chosen not to include a citation for this forum as a subject protection measure.

contributor wrote, "He was proof that the parallel universe existed, as his ideas and observations often revealed a lateral understanding of such breath-taking subtlety of difference, that his universe was clearly only nanoseconds from ours." Sombath was a luminary, widely regarded as one of the top thinkers and planners for Lao development. His disappearance heightened the divide between the parallel universe imagined by Sombath's development partners, a universe in which his programs were successful and he was alive, and contemporary Laos. There was a sense that this other universe— an increasingly liberal and prosperous Laos—was being foreclosed. My point is not to argue for the objective reality of this parallel universe, or the reality of the death space made by state terror, but to examine this sociocultural experience of parallelism. The phenomena of disappearance may produce a sense of laterality—someone is simultaneously dead and alive, or perhaps is alive only in a parallel universe that is made perceptible by hope. "The disappeared are in another world," and it is the precise terror of this form of violence that it threatens "being thrust across a menacing threshold and into a somewhere whose whereabouts and coordinates are unknown and threatening" (Gordon 2008, 63). During the yearly anniversary events on this online forum, contributors post excerpts from his speeches and articles "from Sombath" in the present tense, pretending that he is writing the posts himself. The forum includes an extensive archive of Sombath's publications, videos of his presentations, transcripts of his speeches, and other paraphernalia; animated by this archive of what remains, he is made a potent apparition. The virtuality of the online forum makes it seem possible that he could be posting them, secretly, from the parallel universe where he is still alive.

The disappeared are not dead: "death exists in the past tense, disappearance in the present" (Gordon 2008, 113). The significance of past or present tense can be quite obvious, as when English-language materials handed out by Sombath's friends and family in the wake of his disappearance used both tenses interchangeably: "Sombath's passion is . . . Sombath was . . . he was . . . he was . . . his family is still urging the Lao Government to find him and return him safely" (Sombath.org pamphlet, no date). Disappearance is a form of hauntological power that could be explained in terms of a series of parallels: living and dead, visible and invisible, real and surreal, and past and present without any resolution. It is precisely this haunting that makes disappearance so potent a political act of terror. The phantom figure of the disappeared is key to understanding the ambiguity of the current period of postwar revival, particularly with regard to ongoing war violence and political violence. Antonius C. G. M. Robben argues, in the context of the Argentine Dirty War, that disappearance "extends state terror into the hereafter" (2000, 93). Disappearance deprives kin of the possibility of proper memorialization of the corpse. In predominantly Catholic Argentina, this produced fears that the deceased's surviving soul would not be able or willing to serve as a spiritual resource for the living (for example, that it would be impossible to produce relics of the body). Robben (2000) argues that the Argentine state knowingly intervened into this spiritual process by repressing the process of turning the dead into relics and martyrs. Repressing the finality of death and the certainty of the corpse was a political act carried out in the hereafter. "Disappearance is a state-sponsored method for haunting a population" (Gordon 2008, 131). This is not mere ghostly metaphysics, but repressed contestation over the status of the dead and living. Ghosts can be deeply, profoundly political.

On one of the anniversaries of Sombath's disappearance, a training center that he cofounded hosted a *basi* ceremony in his honor. Notably, basi are rituals of reintegration and healing performed for the living, not the dead. Yet it is also the norm to hold funeral rituals on the anniversary of a relative's death. The nature of Sombath's disappearance means that he is neither quite alive nor quite dead—this posed ritual challenges that the organizers addressed by incorporating elements of both funerary and healing rituals. The basi was performed as a healing, restorative ritual, carried out on the putative anniversary of his disappearance (not his death). In the absence of his physical body or corpse, the basi was intended to give positive merit to Sombath's spirit.

Many development workers and government officials attended the basi "in an unofficial capacity . . . to pay their respects," a colleague told me. She elaborated, "Many people think his spirit is"—she waves her hands loosely above her head—"around and they want to give their merit to him." Sombath's body was never recovered and, therefore, he never received the proper funeral rituals. As I discussed in chapter 2, when a corpse is not recovered whole, or when a deceased person is not properly memorialized, they almost always become an angry ghost. The forced disappearance of Sombath has this additional, spiritual entailment: he has been removed from the pool of productive ancestor spirits and brutally transformed into a destructive ghost. The basi ceremony could be understood, in this logic, as an effort to stabilize Sombath as still among the living and therefore maintain the possibility of his being a positive force. Many of his colleagues feel responsible for this lack of proper memorialization—there is a fear that if he is dead, his ghost is haunting the development sector and is partially responsible for the increasing difficulty of getting projects approved or sourcing funding. The difficulty of carrying out development in the post-Sombath years is taken as evidence of his bad death. Development is haunted by his ghost.

There was uncertainty about the political status of the basi and, therefore, about the safety of the participants. Many of the materials from the event did not include direct reference to Sombath or his disappearance. Enforced disappearance propagates in these little secrets, uncertainties, and half revelations. One had to be in the know to understand the purpose of the event in advance. Bracelets, tokens of the event handed out to guests, were imprinted with the words HOPE/FAITH/COURAGE/STRENGTH but did not include any direct reference to Sombath. Showing me his bracelet, a colleague who attended the event speculated, "They didn't put his name on them—I think they just want it to be a reminder to be strong and courageous, like him."

Most of my colleagues in the development sector didn't go because of this implicit political threat. A lower-level program officer at my host office explained to me, "It is too sensitive, so I didn't go. . . . I think if you go, it means that you want to raise something [with the government]." She examined some of the materials from the event that I had brought to show her, including a pamphlet showing still images from the CCTV footage. She seemed visibly shaken by the images, examining them closely a few inches in front of her face. She and Sombath worked together for several years on a variety of rural development projects.

After a pause, she pointed to the blurry license plate of the van in the image. "The plate number here must mean something—why can't they track it?"

I tell her darkly, "I don't think that is the point." And she turned her body abruptly toward me, as if I had shaken her, and made brief eye contact before returning to scrutinizing the blurry photos.

The Phaseout

My fieldwork was, in a very literal sense, haunted by Sombath's ghost. I never met him personally, but his absence shaped much of my research: I was told, slowly by my interlocutors, of how he had inhabited these same rooms, or driven down these same streets. I opened this conclusion with one of these moments of ghostly revelation, where the checkpoint that I passed every day on the way to my office was suddenly haunted by his absence. I gained research access, or was denied access, in relation to people's assessment of risk in the new post-Sombath period. Many of my interlocutors mused on the time before Sombath disappeared, a time distinguished by more open collaboration between governmental and nongovernmental organizations, when it was supposedly possible to carry out development work with good-will and trust. In these polarizing accounts, this is starkly different from the period after Mr. Sombath, a time in which the government has been actively reassessing the relations between the Party state and its international development partners. As part of this reassessment, the bureaucratic structure of the state has shifted massively, creating or destroying entire departments. The state has refused to authorize any new nonprofit groups and has frozen many project applications and agreements and is, simultaneously, rewriting its regulations with regard to nonprofit and NGO activities.

This high-profile disappearance, and the paranoia that it fomented in the Lao development sector, forced me to revise much of my initially planned fieldwork. I arrived in Laos in June 2012 for three months of preliminary fieldwork. At that time, I set up several research relationships with a number of potential long-term research hosts. Sombath disappeared in December 2012. When I returned to Laos in July 2013, I discovered that many of the research agreements I had made the previous summer needed to be renegotiated for the post-Sombath years. One of these organizations, with which I had negotiated a long-term research position, ultimately decided to rescind their research support entirely. My research liaison was extremely apologetic; he told me that the organization could no longer justify having an American researcher on staff. They were under too much pressure from the government. Every staff member needed to be explained, accounted for, and approved by their government partners. In his opinion, there was no way that a foreign researcher (especially an American) would get this approval. He felt it was risky to even ask—even the intimation of too many foreign connections was rumored dangerous.

As I discussed in chapter 1, I treat these accounts of suppression, paranoia, and violence as evidence for an ethnography of authoritarian power in contemporary Laos. The obstacles that I faced in carrying out this research are evidence of the authoritarian revival that forms a central part of my argument for revivals/remains. As such, I do not recount these events as a form of ethnographic reflexivity in the conventional sense; this is not my version of Bronislaw Malinowski's (1935) "odyssey of blunders" in fieldwork. Experiences of state terror are another hazard of fieldwork, as I described that term in chapter 1. Accounts of state terror can be treated as temporary aberrations in the normal functioning of states, perhaps in response to the violent extremism of a terrorist group or the necessity of asserting national control after war. Following other scholars of terror, I refute this argument and assert, rather, that terror is intrinsic to modern forms of war and power (Masco 2014; Orr 2004; Sluka 2000; Taussig 1987). Engaging these hazards and terrors as constitutive of everyday life foregrounds the importance of ethnographic fieldwork. The ethnographic task is to examine the cultural specificity of these experiences toward the elaboration of the more general sociocultural processes that produce terror.

Another organization that I partnered with modulated our research relationship so that they could provide covert assistance without claiming me as an official staff member. I had originally been selected as a research intern with one of their project teams and had already secured written approval to do so from the organization's country director. In my post-Sombath negotiations with this organization, this offer was rescinded, and I was instead given access to interview team members and read project documents. The country director told me privately that her staff were experiencing tightening bureaucratic restrictions and increased threats from police. During a recent site visit to a rural area, she had been harassed by armed policemen. The previous research intern, whom I was going to replace, had been unable to carry out his research due to these threats and other, less overtly violent, bureaucratic obstacles. In response to this, I recall telling the country director that her choice to limit my research activities was perpetuating the access problem and contributing to a culture of ignorance and fear. At the same time, both of us recognized that she had a responsibility to protect her staff and interns (which, in this case, meant choosing to cancel my internship).

After these repeated limitations or rejections of my research, I was thrilled to receive an offer of research support from another organization that I had been introduced to via my contacts in the victim assistance sector. This international NGO was just beginning to support victim assistance and mine risk education projects in Laos. The organization had been one of Sombath's primary development partners and continued to carry out his legacy by supporting projects in his absence. In their own way, they were familiar with negotiating heightened government surveillance and threat. These staff members also had stories of police harassment and bureaucratic tightening, but these experiences were not treated as ultimate obstacles. The leader of this organization was a scion of a politically influential family in Laos. Program staff prided themselves on being more socially progressive and politically relevant than other foreign development organizations. I was, indeed, still a liability for them; but I was also an asset and a resource for an organization that viewed itself as more socially progressive and politically influential.

Nonetheless, my research hosts were not immune to the increasing challenges of working in Laos. Their local nonprofit partners, for example, had not been able to get any new licenses approved in the three years since Sombath's disappearance. Many of their existing agreements with the government were frozen in bureaucratic deadlock. It was becoming increasingly difficult to partner with local groups or receive authorization for new projects. The growing sense of threat, especially toward foreign staff, was also becoming an obstacle to setting up projects in Laos. Halfway through my primary fieldwork in 2014–15, my host organization announced that they would be phasing out of Laos entirely. The decision was made by the organization's home office in Europe, and none of the local office staff (who were almost entirely Lao) were consulted in the decision-making process. Staff were informed that there were larger financial and programmatic shifts at the home office that, in combination with the increasing challenges of working effectively in Laos, had propelled this decision. My research agreement with them would end just as the organization would be leaving the country.

After the announcement of the phaseout, a high-level staff member told me that "the Sombath issue" was indicative of the current challenges faced by this organization in carrying out its development work. Normally a calm person, his sense of anger was palpable as we talked: "The government refuses to resolve [Sombath's disappearance]," which perpetuates a sense that civil society action is not feasible for others. The "space for civil society and faith has reversed [since Sombath's disappearance]. I would have liked to work in the normal way with a reasonable space for civil society and for [international] NGOs to criticize the government. But that was not the case in Laos, and it is hard to see if it is going to change." Expressing an opinion shared by many of my interlocutors, this man voiced his concern that Sombath's disappearance was an indicator of the increasing hazards of working in Laos: hazards that included the shrinking space for civil society, the closing off of venues for advocating to the government, bureaucratic blockages, and, as projects increasingly stalled, a shrinking of their funding base. From the perspective of many of my colleagues, strained relations between the local and the home office (including the fact that the phaseout decision was made without consulting the local office) were yet another hazard of working in Laos. In my discussions with my colleagues at this organization, I felt a parallel between the phaseout and my own experiences of research hazard. The term "phaseout" became evocative of our shared concerns over authoritarian revival and the practicalities of working under conditions of repression and fear. In this context, it came to seem fitting that I was leaving Laos at the same time as my host organization was phasing out.

As more staff left, and more projects were shut down or handed off to other development partners, the feeling in the office darkened and tightened. There was a potent sense of things being closed off, or cut off. Staff meetings, which had previously often been friendly affairs, became melancholic. I was increasingly asked to sit out of meetings when things got too personal, or made the choice to leave of my own accord out of respect for what felt like funerary proceedings for someone else's family. My hosts asked me to help them go through their expansive physical archive, spanning their initial field research in Laos in the 1980s and ending with the shutting down of their most recent projects. My task was to sort through everything and identify what was worth keeping (sending to other development organizations or government partners, or sending to the home office's archive abroad). Going through the archive acquired the viscerality of conducting an autopsy. The moldering papers, slowly decomposing in the tropical air, covered my fingers with dark powdery stains. Some of the typewritten pages of yellowing paper felt as fragile as grave wrappings. This task also gave me the opportunity to request to keep any materials that I wanted for my research—the country director's parting gift. Prior to the announcement of the phaseout, I had been conducting an institutional history of the organization; suddenly, I found myself in the position, also, of documenting its death.

Writing against Terror

In chapter 1, I described my fieldwork as a kind of "fingers crossed ethnography" (Calvey 2008, 913) in which the success of my research was uncomfortably dependent on my ability to navigate the hazards of conducting research under an authoritarian regime. Near the end of my fieldwork, as I was wrapping up long-term interview partnerships and securing copies of archival documents from my hosts, the secretary at one of my host offices got a call from the airport police. They had found a bag with my name on it and wanted me to come pick it up. I had not been to the airport in nearly four months and was not missing anything. The secretary, a friend of mine, cautioned me that it was very odd that they knew to call for me at the office (since I was not employed there). She told me to ignore the call and not to go to the airport. My other friends were more forceful: Don't go. They believed it was a ruse to try to arrest me on fake drug charges. I took this advice and did not follow up with the police about my missing bag. A few weeks later, when I went to the airport for my departing flight out of Laos, I made sure that an older Lao friend accompanied me to the gate—at the very least, so that I would not present myself as a foreigner alone to the attentions of the airport police. Other than needing to negotiate a fee with the border officer, the departure was uneventful.

This instance with the missing bag was one among many when I felt open "the door of the uncanny, the door of the fragment, the door of the shocking parallel" into which people disappear (Gordon 2008, 66). I present these uncanny experiences in this conclusion to adapt my theorization of parallel remains/revivals into an invitation to the anthropological study of military waste. The routinization of police harassment perpetuated a sense of constantly being on the threshold of another, more brutal world. Placing one's feet on this threshold carried the dual injunction to engage the threat of violence and, more profoundly, to live one's life as if there was no threat. How might we, as researchers, address these experiences of parallelism in our research? And what might this add to our hazardous research methods tool kit? I have addressed these questions and concerns by developing parallelism as a conceptual, ethical, and methodological frame for my research. The present analysis of disappearance is my final elaboration of this conceptual frame.

Anthropologists of terror have argued for the need to "write against terror" in their scholarship (Sluka 2000; Taussig 1987). My particular approach involves not only producing politically complex and morally compelling scholarship, but, as I discussed in the introduction and in chapter 3, also paying very careful attention to the reader's experience with a text. As I discussed in the introduction, I have approached this injunction by cultivating a sense of incompleteness and irresolution in my writing, most noticeably by including a bare minimum of subject identifiers for my interlocutors. Sombath Somphone is the only subject's name that I reveal—as a counterpoint to his absence; as a claim about the paradoxical solidity of disappearance as it shapes social reality; and in recognition of the low risks associated with revealing the name of a high-profile public figure presumed dead. In this manner, I am embedding some part of my theoretical claims in the format of my book and style of my writing—to be activated in the reader as she experiences the text. My goal through this process has been to develop methods and writing styles that better research and represent the experience of fraught postwar revival. This involves reassessing what counts as data and description—I have employed modes of thin description and fieldpoetry in my personal effort to write against terror.

My proposal for an anthropology of military waste is another response to the injunction to write against terror—where military waste is one among many possible terrors (or hazards, in the vocabulary of this book) in postwar zones. I make this proposition as a means of orienting my current and future work and as an invitation to future work by other scholars interested in the anthropology of military waste. My analysis of the specific social and cultural impact of military waste in Laos contributes to the development of a meaningful and robust analytic for researching the social and cultural impact of hazards more generally. This book contributes to current interest in the entanglement of disasters and economic development, what Naomi Klein (2007) terms disaster capitalism (see also Adams 2013). This phenomenon also includes the development of an international humanitarian sector after the collapse of the Soviet Union and the opening of many Cold War battlefields to Western intervention—a lineage that includes the development of humanitarian explosives clearance operators. Writing on a modern militarized humanitarianism, Didier Fassin and Mariella Pandolfi argue that "disasters and conflicts are now embedded in the same global logic of intervention" (2010, 10; see also Redfield 2013). Military waste zones are crucial sites of both military and humanitarian intervention. The present study is part of a much larger scholarly project to research and engage with the transformation of war zones into economically productive states—including the study of the organizations and processes that facilitate these transformations.

Military waste provokes an analysis of the parallelism of ecological contamination and geopolitical conflict, for which there is no strict divide between state violence and other forms of hazard. The focus of analysis, as I discuss in the introduction, is on the process of wasting itself as simultaneously geopolitical and ecological. This involves assessing how traces of past violence persist, producing subtle or unintended effects in places that are technically no longer active war zones. In my broader use of the concept of hazard, there are meaningful correspondences between the terror of disappearing and the terror of exploding. I am not arguing that military waste zones inevitably contain the specific terrors of political disappearance; rather, I am arguing for a parallel logic of violence in which hazards develop side by side, layering without necessarily intersecting. An anthropology of military waste might, in a similar manner, approach the broader processes of wasting, endangerment, militarization, and terrorization within and beyond strictly bordered clearance zones. To the extent that anthropology is a humanist discipline, ethics might serve as a border-marking practice for this emerging field of research and researchers. Anthropologists have generally encountered and studied military waste in the course of pursuing research on unrelated topics—to the extent that military waste is already present in their field sites. This field will continue to develop as anthropologists respond to the potent dynamics of loss, grief, and hope that characterize conflict zones and people's interactions with remains of war.

Closing Invocation

"Why would they decide to bomb this?"

She gestures with her arm out to a group of buffalo grazing by the side of the road; one raises its huge gray, bristled head and mews at us as we pass. The wooden bells at their necks create a soft percussion, a sound so familiar in these villages that it is nearly synonymous with the wind and the birds. Her gesture encompasses the fields beyond, a patchwork of rice paddies in the process of second planting before harvest. It is late afternoon and the low sun draws out the bright yellow-green of the young rice shoots, glowing nearly neon with life. The shoots are bundled in the fields, tied with strips of bamboo so that they lean into each other in preparation for being replanted—the farmers have left and there are no people visible. Between the fields are stilt houses with corrugated iron or grass-thatch roofs and walls made of woven bamboo. The low sun paints long spider-leg shadows behind each stilt house. Every door a dark rectangle, deceptively empty.

Her arm completes its gesture and returns to her lap, clenched. She turns again toward me and leans in slightly. Her eyes wander over my face, searching. There is a pause, then she says, "I sometimes think that this is World War III. And people decided to end the war in 1975, but it didn't end." She shakes her head a little. "People are still *dying* and the bombs are still *here*. The war is not over; only the paperwork is finished."

I feel her words drop into the pit of my stomach like a thing that can't be eaten. Embracing her cynicism is like swallowing a thing that is still alive. Working through this effect upon myself, I can think of nothing to say to her in response. My Lao interlocutor was born in a heavily contaminated province and now works in another heavily contaminated province as a risk educator for a major international explosives clearance operator. The paperwork that she is referencing is the forms that must be signed at the end of a risk education workshop to certify that the workshop was completed. The forms mark the official end of each project, without at all marking the end of danger, risk, or violence. She is roughly the same age as me—we were both born after the war—but this thin affinity does not fill the space between us. Sometimes, the only possible response is silence, shared.

FIELDPOEM 18
Children

Luk laberd
bomb children

How do we know our mothers?
If they destroy themselves

her shaking, her falling down
opens herself, her labor
her hollowness without childhood

Seven hundred dropped near the village water pump

Appendix. Notes on Fieldpoems

FIELDPOEM 30: *Postwar*

After completing fieldwork, I returned to my native California. I wrote this poem on the Amtrak train from Oakland to a family gathering in Fresno— the train passed by military training grounds, farm fields abandoned due to the extreme drought, protest signs claiming local water rights, laborers bent double picking fruit, shantytowns, strip malls, and new housing complexes on the expanding edge of suburbia. This was the last fieldpoem I wrote during research.

FIELDPOEM 11: *The Fruit Eaters*

Cluster submunitions, the most common type of military waste in Laos, are called by the names of the fruits they most resemble. People often encounter bombs while foraging for wild foods in the forests surrounding their villages. The title of the poem is a reference to fruit eaters, a Theravada Buddhist name for beings who exit the cycles of violence that characterize our world by practicing virtuous eating habits. In a special paradise realm, these merit-filled people eat only fruit that falls from wild trees. Such food is free from karmic entailments (e.g., the bad karma of slaughtering animals). I heard this analogy frequently enough from villagers and clearance technicians that it stuck in my mind, long before I had made the connection to the Buddhist realm of the fruit eaters. Adding poignant depth to the analogy, many kinds of cluster submunitions look like wild fruits. The clearance technician quoted in the poem wonders if American weapons experts had studied Lao native fruits in order to make their bombs especially insidious. This poem won an Ethnographic Poetry Prize from the Society for Humanistic Anthropology.

FIELDPOEM 15: *"The Rice Is More Delicious after Bomb Clearance"*

Risk education trainers teach Lao farmers to use shovels (instead of hoes or other overhand tools) because they are less likely to trigger explosions. If an explosion does occur, upper-body impairments (such as blindness) are most common. I once heard a Buddhist meditation in which novices were encouraged to treasure the rice in their alms bowl as if each two grains were as precious as their two eyes. The title quote is from a farmer interviewed for a postclearance assessment conducted by one of my colleagues.

FIELDPOEM 23: *Blast Radius*

I wrote this poem shortly after fieldwork with a bomb clearance team completing demolition of a cache of nearly fifty pieces of ordnance: mostly cluster bomblets, but also about a dozen rocket-propelled grenades and several large rockets. Intriguingly, the rockets still had their caps on, meaning that they were never used in battle or were misfired. The field manager was using an unfamiliar, wireless trigger mechanism to destroy these remnants of war, and the first several triggers were unsuccessful due to operator error—thus, there is no explosion in the poem. This poem won an Ethnographic Poetry Prize from the Society for Humanistic Anthropology.

FIELDPOEM 26: *House Blessings*

In the lowlands of Laos, where most people are Theravada Buddhist, it is common for monks and nuns to leave their temples to perform house blessings in private homes near the temple. These private rituals, usually centering around the chanting of sacred texts, are performed with the goal of nurturing household health, happiness, and prosperity. House blessings may also be invoked to dispel bad spirits or ghosts that are causing misfortune for living family members.

FIELDPOEM 18: *Children*

In Lao, cluster munitions are often called *mee laberd* (bomb mothers) and the cluster submunitions inside called *luk laberd* (bomb children). The action of being dropped from the plane forces the bomb mother open, deploying hundreds or thousands of smaller bomb children over vast areas below. I first heard this set of phrases while conducting fieldwork with an explosives clearance team surveying a rice field. An older Lao bomb technician was carefully digging up a BLU-26 cluster submunition with his hands and a small trowel. He called me over and pulled aside a flowering bush to show me the small, rusty sphere of bomb half submerged in the gray soil. "Ni meen luk laberd." Here is a bomb child.

References

Adams, Vincanne. 2013. *Markets of Sorrow, Labors of Faith: New Orleans in the Wake of Katrina*. Durham, NC: Duke University Press.

Ahmed, Sara. 2017. *Living a Feminist Life*. Durham, NC: Duke University Press.

Anderson, Benedict. 1990. *Language and Power: Exploring Political Cultures in Indonesia*. Ithaca, NY: Cornell University Press.

Anderson, Benedict. 1998. *The Spectre of Comparisons*. New York: Verso.

Aretxaga, Begona. 2000. "A Fictional Reality: Paramilitary Death Squads and the Construction of State Terror in Spain." In *Death Squad: The Anthropology of State Terror*, edited by Jeffrey A. Sluka, 46–69. Philadelphia: University of Pennsylvania Press.

Askew, Marc, William Logan, and Colin Long. 2006. *Vientiane: Lao Urbanism, Memory and Identity*. Asia's Transformations. London: Routledge.

Baird, Ian G., and Philippe Le Billon. 2012. "Landscapes of Political Memories: War Legacies and Land Negotiations in Laos." *Political Geography* 31 (5): 290–300.

Benda, Harry J. 1962. "The Structure of Southeast Asian History: Some Preliminary Observations." *Journal of Southeast Asian History* 3 (1): 106–38.

Bennett, Jane. 2010. *Vibrant Matter: A Political Ecology of Things*. Durham, NC: Duke University Press.

Bernard, H. Russell. 2011. *Research Methods in Anthropology: Qualitative and Quantitative Approaches*. 5th ed. Lanham, MD: AltaMira.

Boas, Franz. 1919. "Scientists as Spies." *The Nation*, December 20, 797.

Boddington, Michael A. B., and Bountao Chanthavongsa. 2008. *National Survey of UXO Victims and Accidents: Phase 1*. Vientiane: National Regulatory Authority for UXO/Mine Action Sector Lao PDR (NRA).

Branfman, Fred. 2013. *Voices from the Plain of Jars: Life under an Air War*. 2nd ed. Madison: University of Wisconsin Press.

Calvey, David. 2008. "The Art and Politics of Covert Research: Doing 'Situated Ethics' in the Field." *Sociology* 42 (5): 905–18. doi:10.1177/0038038508094569.

Coates, Karen J., and Jerry Redfern. 2013. *Eternal Harvest: The Legacy of American Bombs in Laos*. San Francisco: Things Asian/Global Directions.

Collins, Steven. 1997. "The Body in Theravāda Buddhist Monasticism." In *Religion and the Body*, edited by Sarah Coakley, 185–204. Cambridge: Cambridge University Press.

Convention on Cluster Munitions. 2008. United Nations Development Program, Dublin, May 30. http://www.clusterconvention.org.

Cooper, Robert. 2014. *Laos: Work in Progress*. Vientiane: Lao Insight.

Daniel, E. Valentine. 1996. *Charred Lullabies: Chapters in an Anthropology of Violence*. Princeton Studies in Culture/Power/History. Princeton, NJ: Princeton University Press.

Darwish, Mahmoud. 1995. *Memory for Forgetfulness: August, Beirut, 1982*. Translated by Ibrahim Muhawi. Berkeley: University of California Press.

Daughtry, J. Martin. 2015. *Listening to War: Sound, Music, Trauma, and Survival in Wartime Iraq*. Oxford: Oxford University Press.

Davies, James. 2010. "Disorientation, Dissonance, and Altered Perception in the Field." In *Emotions in the Field: The Psychology and Anthropology of Fieldwork Experience*, edited by James Davies and Spencer Dimitrina, 47–66. Stanford, CA: Stanford University Press.

Davies, James, and Dimitrina Spencer, eds. 2010. *Emotions in the Field: The Psychology and Anthropology of Fieldwork Experience*. Stanford, CA: Stanford University Press.

Davis, Colin. 2013. "État Présent: Hauntology, Spectres and Phantoms." In *The Spectralities Reader: Ghosts and Haunting in Contemporary Cultural Theory*, edited by Maria del Pilar Blanco and Esther Peeren, 53–60. New York: Bloomsbury Academic.

Deleuze, Gilles. 1994. *Difference and Repetition*. New York: Columbia University Press.

Deleuze, Gilles, and Félix Guattari. 1987. *A Thousand Plateaus: Capitalism and Schizophrenia*. Minneapolis: University of Minnesota Press.

del Pilar Blanco, Maria, and Esther Peeren. 2013. "Introduction: Conceptualizing Spectralities." In *The Spectralities Reader: Ghosts and Haunting in Contemporary Cultural Theory*, edited by Maria del Pilar Blanco and Esther Peeren, 1–28. New York: Bloomsbury Academic.

Derrida, Jacques. (1993) 2006. *Specters of Marx: The State of Debt, the Work of Mourning and the New International*. Routledge Classics. New York: Routledge.

Derrida, Jacques, Terry Eagleton, Frederic Jameson, Antonio Negri, et al. 1999. *Ghostly Demarcations: A Symposium on Jacques Derrida's Spectres of Marx*. Edited by Michael Sprinker. London: Verso.

Derrida, Jacques, and Bernard Steigler. 2013. "Spectrographies." In *The Spectralities Reader: Ghosts and Haunting in Contemporary Cultural Theory*, edited by Maria del Pilar Blanco and Esther Peeren, 37–52. New York: Bloomsbury Academic.

Elyachar, Julia. 2012a. "Before (and after) Neoliberalism: Tacit Knowledge, Secrets of the Trade, and the Public Sector in Egypt." *Cultural Anthropology* 27 (1): 76–96.

Elyachar, Julia. 2012b. "Next Practices: Knowledge, Infrastructure, and Public Goods at the Bottom of the Pyramid." *Public Culture* 24 (1 66): 109–29. doi:10.1215/08992363-1443583.

Erlmann, Veit. 2014. *Reason and Resonance: A History of Modern Aurality*. New York: Zone.

Errington, Shelly. 1989. *Meaning and Power in a Southeast Asian Realm*. Princeton, NJ: Princeton University Press.

Errington, Shelly. 1990. "Recasting Sex, Gender, and Power: A Theoretical and Regional Overview." In *Power and Difference: Gender in Island Southeast Asia*, edited by Shelly Errington and J. Atkinson, 1–58. Stanford, CA: Stanford University Press.

Evans, Grant. 1990. *Lao Peasants under Socialism*. New Haven, CT: Yale University Press.

Evans, Grant. 1998. *The Politics of Ritual and Remembrance: Laos since 1975*. Honolulu: University of Hawai'i Press.

Evans, Grant. 2004. "Laos: Situation Analysis and Trend Assessment." A Writenet Report commissioned by United Nations High Commissioner for Refugees, Protection Information Section. May.

Fassin, Didier. 2012. *Humanitarian Reason: A Moral History of the Present*. Berkeley: University of California Press.

Fassin, Didier, and Mariella Pandolfi. 2010. "Introduction: Military and Humanitarian Government in the Age of Intervention." In *Contemporary States of Emergency: The Politics of Military and Humanitarian Interventions*, edited by Didier Fassin and Mariella Pandolfi, 9–28. New York: Zone.

Faulkner, Sandra L. 2009. *Poetry as Method: Reporting Research through Verse*. Walnut Creek, CA: Left Coast.

Feld, Steven. 2012. *Sound and Sentiment: Birds, Weeping, Poetics, and Song in Kaluli Expression*. 3rd ed. Durham, NC: Duke University Press.

Forsey, Martin Gerard. 2010. "Ethnography as Participant Listening." *Ethnography* 11 (4): 558–72.

Fox, James J. 1971. "Semantic Parallelism in Rotinese Ritual Language." *Bijdragen tot de Taal-, Land- en Volkenkunde* 127 (2): 215–55.

Fox, James J. 1974. "'Our Ancestors Spoke in Pairs': Rotinese Views of Language, Dialect, and Code." In *Explorations in the Ethnography of Speaking*, edited by Richard Bauman and Joel Sherzer, 65–85. Cambridge: Cambridge University Press.

Frank, Pat. 2013. *Alas, Babylon*. New York: Harper Collins.

French, Lindsay. 1994. "The Political Economy of Injury and Compassion: Amputees on the Thai-Cambodia Border." In *Embodiment and Experience: The Existential Ground of Culture and Self*, edited by Thomas J. Csordas, 69–99. Cambridge: Cambridge University Press.

Gammeltoft, Tine M. 2014. "Toward an Anthropology of the Imaginary: Specters of Disability in Vietnam." *Ethos* 42 (2): 153–74. doi:10.1111/etho.12046.

Geertz, Clifford. 1973. *The Interpretation of Cultures*. New York: Basic Books.

Geertz, Clifford. 1983. *Local Knowledge*. 3rd ed. New York: Basic Books.

Good, Byron J. 2015. "Haunted by Aceh: Specters of Violence in Post-Suharto Indonesia." In *Genocide and Mass Violence: Memory, Symptom, and Recovery*, edited by David Hinton and Alexander L. Hinton, 58–82. Cambridge: Cambridge University Press.

Goodman, Steve. 2012. *Sonic Warfare: Sound, Affect, and the Ecology of Fear*. Cambridge, MA: MIT Press.

Gordon, Avery. 2008. *Ghostly Matters: Haunting and the Sociological Imagination*. New University of Minnesota Press ed. Minneapolis: University of Minnesota Press.

Goscha, Christopher, and Sören Ivarson, eds. 2003. *Contesting Visions of the Lao Past: Lao Historiography at a Crossroads.* Copenhagen: NIAS Press.

Gun, Geoffrey C. 1998. *Theravadins, Colonialists and Commissars in Laos.* Bangkok: White Lotus.

Gustafsson, Mai Lan. 2009. *War and Shadows: The Haunting of Vietnam.* Ithaca, NY: Cornell University Press.

Hansen, Anne R. 2007. *How to Behave: Buddhism and Modernity in Colonial Cambodia, 1860–1930.* Southeast Asia: Politics, Meaning, and Memory. Honolulu: University of Hawai'i Press.

Hansen, Mette H. 2006. "In the Footsteps of the Communist Party: Dilemmas and Strategies." In *Doing Fieldwork in China*, edited by Maria Heimer and Stig Thogersen, 81–95. Copenhagen: NIAS Press.

Haraway, Donna J. 2003. *The Companion Species Manifesto: Dogs, People, and Significant Otherness.* Vol. 1. Chicago: Prickly Paradigm.

Helmreich, Stefan. 2015. "Transduction." In *Keywords in Sound*, edited by David Novak and Matt Sakakeeny, 222–31. Durham, NC: Duke University Press.

Helmreich, Stefan. 2016. *Sounding the Limits of Life: Essays in the Anthropology of Biology and Beyond.* Princeton, NJ: Princeton University Press.

Henig, David. 2012. "Iron in the Soil: Living with Military Waste in Bosnia-Herzegovina." *Anthropology Today* 28 (1): 21–23.

High, Holly. 2011. "Melancholia and Anthropology." *American Ethnologist* 38 (2): 217–33. doi:10.1111/j.1548–1425.2011.01302.x.

High, Holly. 2014. *Fields of Desire: Poverty and Policy in Laos.* Singapore: National University of Singapore Press.

High, Holly, James R. Curran, and Gareth Robinson. 2013. "Electronic Records of the Air War over Southeast Asia: A Database Analysis." *Journal of Vietnamese Studies* 8 (4): 86–124.

Hirschkind, Charles. 2015. "Religion." In *Keywords in Sound*, edited by David Novak and Matt Sakakeeny, 165–74. Durham, NC: Duke University Press.

Hirshfield, Jane. 2015. *Ten Windows: How Great Poems Transform the World.* New York: Knopf.

Holt, John Clifford. 2009. *Spirits of the Place: Buddhism and Lao Religious Culture.* Honolulu: University of Hawai'i Press.

Ingold, Tim. 2011. *Being Alive: Essays on Movement, Knowledge and Description.* London: Routledge.

Jackson, John L., Jr. 2013. *Thin Description: Ethnography and the African Hebrew Israelites of Jerusalem.* Cambridge, MA: Harvard University Press.

Jacobs, Seth. 2012. *The Universe Unravelling: American Foreign Policy in Cold War Laos.* Ithaca, NY: Cornell University Press.

Jakobson, Roman. 1966. "Grammatical Parallelism and Its Russian Facet." *Language* 42 (2): 399–429. doi:10.2307/411699.

Jameson, Fredric. 1999. "Marx's Purloined Letter." In *Ghostly Demarcations: A Symposium on Jacques Derrida's Spectres of Marx*, edited by Michael Sprinker, 29–67. London: Verso.

Johnson, Andrew A. 2014. *Ghosts of the New City: Spirits, Urbanity, and the Ruins of Progress in Chiang Mai*. Honolulu: University of Hawai'i Press.

Keane, Webb. 1997. *Signs of Recognition: Powers and Hazards of Representation in an Indonesian Society*. Berkeley: University of California Press.

Kim, Eleana. 2016. "Toward an Anthropology of Landmines: Rogue Infrastructure and Military Waste in the Korean DMZ." *Cultural Anthropology* 13 (2): 162–87. doi:10.14506/ca31.2.02.

Klein, Naomi. 2007. *The Shock Doctrine: The Rise of Disaster Capitalism*. New York: Metropolitan.

Klima, Alan. 2002. *The Funeral Casino: Meditation, Massacre, and Exchange with the Dead in Thailand*. Princeton, NJ: Princeton University Press.

Koret, Peter. 1999. "Books of Search: The Invention of Traditional Lao Literature as a Subject of Study." In *Laos: Culture and Society*, edited by Grant Evans, 226–57. Chiang Mai: Silkworm.

Koret, Peter. 2000. "Books of Search: Convention and Creativity in Traditional Lao Literature." In *The Canon in Southeast Asian Literatures*, edited by David Smyth, 210–33. London: Routledge.

Kurlantzick, Joshua. 2017. *A Great Place to Have a War: America in Laos and the Birth of a Military CIA*. New York: Simon and Schuster.

Kwon, Heonik. 2008. *Ghosts of War in Vietnam*. Cambridge: Cambridge University Press.

Ladwig, Patrice. 2013. "Ontology, Materiality and Spectral Traces: Methodological Thoughts on Studying Lao Buddhist Festivals for Ghosts and Ancestral Spirits." *Anthropological Theory* 12 (4): 427–47. doi:10.1177/1463499612471933.

Ladwig, Patrice. 2015. "Worshipping Relics and Animating Statues: Transformations of Buddhist Statecraft in Contemporary Laos." *Modern Asian Studies* 49 (6): 1875–1902. doi:10.1017/S0026749X13000486.

Latour, Bruno. 1993. *We Have Never Been Modern*. Cambridge, MA: Harvard University Press.

LCMM. 2017. "Lao PDR: Mine Ban Policy." *Landmine and Cluster Munition Monitor*, October 26, 2017. www.the-monitor.org/en-gb/reports/2017/lao-pdr/mine-ban-policy .aspx.

Leavy, Patricia. 2009. *Method Meets Art: Arts-Based Research Practice*. New York: Guilford.

Lee-Treweek, Geraldine, and Stephanie Linkogle, eds. 2000. *Danger in the Field: Risk and Ethics in Social Research*. London: Routledge.

Lewis, Martin W., and Kären E. Wigen. 1997. *The Myth of Continents: A Critique of Metageography*. Berkeley: University of California Press.

Love, Heather. 2013. "Close Reading and Thin Description." *Public Culture* 25 (3): 401–34. doi:10.1215/08992363-2144688.

Malabou, Catherine. 2012. *The Ontology of the Accident: An Essay on Destructive Plasticity*. Translated by Carolyn Shread. Cambridge: Polity Press, 2012.

Malinowski, Bronislaw. 1935. *Coral Gardens and Their Magic: A Study of the Methods of Tilling the Soil and of Agricultural Rites in the Trobriand Islands*. Reprint. New York: American Book.

Masco, Joseph. 2014. *The Theater of Operations: National Security Affect from the Cold War to the War on Terror*. Durham, NC: Duke University Press.

Maurer, Bill. 2005. *Mutual Life, Limited: Islamic Banking, Alternative Currencies, Lateral Reason*. Princeton, NJ: Princeton University Press.

Maxwell, Joseph A. 1996. *Qualitative Research Design: An Interactive Approach*. Thousand Oaks, CA: Sage.

Mayes, Warren, and Nigel Chang. 2014. "Discovering Sepon: Cultural Heritage Management and the Making of a Modern Mine." *Extractive Industries and Society* 1 (2): 237–48. doi:10.1016/j.exis.2014.05.002.

Mbembe, Achille. 2003. "Necropolitics." *Public Culture* 15 (1): 11–40.

Mbembe, Achille. 2013. "From 'Life, Sovereignty, and Terror in the Fiction of Amos Tutuola.'" In *The Spectralities Reader: Ghosts and Haunting in Contemporary Cultural Theory*, edited by Maria del Pilar Blanco and Esther Peeren, 131–50. New York: Bloomsbury Academic.

McCoy, Alfred W. 2013. "Foreword: Reflections on History's Longest Air War." In *Voices from the Plain of Jars: Life under an Air War*, edited by Fred Branfman, 2nd ed., ix–xvi. Madison: University of Wisconsin Press.

Mills, Mara. 2015. "Deafness." In *Keywords in Sound*, edited by David Novak and Matt Sakakeeny, 45–54. Durham, NC: Duke University Press.

MMG. 2016. "Media Release: MMG LXML Sepon Boosts Lao UXO Technicians." Minerals and Metals Group, September 1. Vientiane: MMG LXML.

Nancy, Jean-Luc. 2007. *Listening*. New York: Fordham University Press.

Navaro-Yashin, Yael. 2012. *The Make-Believe Space: Affective Geography in a Postwar Polity*. Durham, NC: Duke University Press.

Nixon, Rob. 2006–7. "Slow Violence, Gender, and the Environmentalism of the Poor." *Journal of Commonwealth and Postcolonial Studies* 13 (2): 14–37.

Nordstrom, Carolyn. 1997. *A Different Kind of War Story*. Philadelphia: University of Pennsylvania Press.

Nordstrom, Carolyn. 2004. *Shadows of War: Violence, Power, and International Profiteering in the Twenty-First Century*. Berkeley: University of California Press.

Nordstrom, Carolyn, and Antonius C. G. M. Robben, eds. 1996. *Fieldwork under Fire: Contemporary Studies of Violence and Culture*. Berkeley: University of California Press.

NPA. 2014. *Cluster Munition Remnants: Methods of Survey and Clearance*. Oslo: Norwegian People's Aid.

NRA. 2010. *The Unexploded Ordnance (UXO) Problem and Operational Progress in the Lao PDR: Official Figures*. Vientiane: National Regulatory Authority for UXO/Mine Action.

Ochoa Gautier, Ana María. 2015. "Silence." In *Keywords in Sound*, edited by David Novak and Matt Sakakeeny, 183–92. Durham, NC: Duke University Press.

Orr, Jackie. 2004. "The Militarization of Inner Space." *Critical Sociology* 30 (2): 451–81.

Pedersen, David. 2012. *Migrants, Money, and Meaning in El Salvador and the United States*. Chicago: University of Chicago Press.

Petit, Pierre. 2013. "The Backstage of Ethnography as Ethnography of the State: Coping with Officials in the Lao People's Democratic Republic." In *Red Stamps and Gold*

Stars, edited by Sarah Turner, 143–64. Vancouver: University of British Colombia Press.

Pholsena, Vatthana. 2006. *Post-war Laos: The Politics of Culture, History, and Identity*. Ithaca, NY: Cornell University Press.

Pholsena, Vatthana. 2013. "A Social Reading of a Post-conflict Landscape: Route 9 in Southern Laos." In *Interactions with a Violent Past: Reading Post-conflict Landscapes in Cambodia, Laos, and Vietnam*, edited by Vatthana Pholsena and Oliver Tappe, 157–85. Singapore: National University of Singapore.

Phraxayavong, Viliam. 2009. *History of Aid to Laos: Motivations and Impacts*. Chiang Mai, Thailand: Mekong.

Ponesse, Julie. 2014. "The Ties That Blind: Conceptualizing Anonymity." *Journal of Social Philosophy* 45 (3): 304–22.

Prendergast, Monica. 2009. "Introduction: The Phenomena of Poetry in Research." In *Poetic Inquiry: Vibrant Voices in the Social Sciences*, edited by Monica Prendergast, Carl Leggo, and Pauline Sameshima, xix–xlii. Rotterdam: Sense.

Puar, Jasbir K. 2017. *The Right to Maim: Debility, Capacity, Disability*. Durham, NC: Duke University Press.

Redfield, Peter. 2005. "Doctors, Borders, and Life in Crisis." *Cultural Anthropology* 20 (3): 328–61.

Redfield, Peter. 2013. *Life in Crisis: The Ethical Journey of Doctors without Borders*. Berkeley: University of California Press.

Reed, Kristin, and Ausra Padskocimaite. 2012. *The Right Toolkit: Applying Research Methods in the Service of Human Rights*. Berkeley: Human Rights Center.

Reid, Anthony J. S. 1993. *Southeast Asia in the Age of Commerce, 1450–1680*. New Haven, CT: Yale University Press.

Reid, Anthony J. S. 1999. "A Saucer Model of Southeast Asian Identity." *Southeast Asian Journal of Social Science* 27 (1): 7–23.

Robben, Antonius C. G. M. 2000. "State Terror in the Netherworld: Disappearance and Reburial in Argentina." In *Death Squad: The Anthropology of State Terror*, edited by Jeffrey A. Sluka, 91–113. Philadelphia: University of Pennsylvania Press.

Rosenblatt, Adam. 2015. *Digging for the Disappeared: Forensic Science after Atrocity*. Stanford, CA: Stanford University Press.

Russell, Elaine. 2013. "Laos—Living with Unexploded Ordnance: Past Memories and Present Realities." In *Interactions with a Violent Past: Reading Post-conflict Landscapes in Cambodia, Laos, and Vietnam*, edited by Vatthana Pholsena and Oliver Tappe, 96–134. Singapore: National University of Singapore Press.

Schober, Juliane. 2010. *Modern Buddhist Conjunctures in Myanmar: Cultural Narratives, Colonial Legacies, and Civil Society*. 2nd ed. Honolulu: University of Hawai'i Press.

Sedgwick, Eve Kosofsky. 2002. "Paranoid Reading and Reparative Reading, or, You're So Paranoid, You Probably Think This Essay Is about You." In *Touching Feeling: Affect, Pedagogy, Performativity*, 123–52. Durham, NC: Duke University Press.

Shread, Carolyn. 2009. Translator's preface to Catherine Malabou, *The Ontology of the Accident: An Essay on Destructive Plasticity*, vii–ix. Cambridge: Polity Press, 2012.

Simpson, Audra. 2014. *Mohawk Interruptus: Political Life across the Borders of Settler States*. Durham, NC: Duke University Press.

Singh, Sarinda. 2012. *Natural Potency and Political Power: Forests and State Authority in Contemporary Laos*. Honolulu: University of Hawai'i Press.

Singh, Sarinda. 2014. "Religious Resurgence, Authoritarianism, and 'Ritual Governance': Baci Rituals, Village Meetings, and the Developmental State in Rural Laos." *Journal of Asian Studies* 73 (4): 1059–79. doi:10.1017/S0021911814001041.

Sluka, Jeffrey A. 2000. "Introduction: State Terror and Anthropology." In *Death Squad: The Anthropology of State Terror*, edited by Jeffrey A. Sluka, 1–45. Philadelphia: University of Pennsylvania Press.

Smail, John R. 1961. "On the Possibility of an Autonomous History of Modern Southeast Asia." *Journal of Southeast Asian History* 2 (2): 72–102.

Smith, Mark M. 2015. "Echo." In *Keywords in Sound*, edited by David Novak and Matt Sakakeeny, 55–64. Durham, NC: Duke University Press.

Stengers, Isabelle. 2012. "Reclaiming Animism." *e-flux Journal*, no. 36 (July). https://www.e-flux.com/journal/36/61245/reclaiming-animism/.

Sterne, Jonathan. 2015. "Hearing." In *Keywords in Sound*, edited by David Novak and Matt Sakakeeny, 65–77. Durham, NC: Duke University Press.

Stoler, Ann Laura. 2013. "'The Rot Remains': From Ruins to Ruination." In *Imperial Debris: On Ruins and Ruination*, edited by Ann Laura Stoler, 1–38. Durham, NC: Duke University Press.

Strathern, Marilyn. 2004. *Partial Connections*. Updated ed. Walnut Creek, CA: AltaMira.

Stuart-Fox, Martin. 1996. *Buddhist Kingdom, Marxist State: The Making of Modern Laos*. Bangkok: White Lotus.

Stuart-Fox, Martin. 1997. *A History of Laos*. Cambridge: Cambridge University Press.

Tambiah, Stanley Jeyaraja. 1976. *World Conqueror and World Renouncer: A Study of Buddhism and Polity in Thailand against a Historical Background*. Cambridge: Cambridge University Press.

Tambiah, Stanley Jeyaraja. 1984. *The Buddhist Saints of the Forest and the Cult of Amulets: A Study in Charisma, Hagiography, Sectarianism, and Millennial Buddhism*. Cambridge: Cambridge University Press.

Tanabe, Shigeharu. 2002. "The Person in Transformation: Body, Mind and Cultural Appropriation." In *Cultural Crisis and Social Memory: Modernity and Identity in Thailand and Laos*, edited by Charles F. Keyes and Shigeharu Tanabe, 43–67. Honolulu: University of Hawai'i Press.

Tappe, Oliver, and Vatthana Pholsena. 2013. "The 'American War,' Post-conflict Landscapes, and Violent Memories." In *Interactions with a Violent Past: Reading Post-conflict Landscapes in Cambodia, Laos, and Vietnam*, edited by Vatthana Pholsena and Oliver Tappe, 1–18. Singapore: National University of Singapore.

Taussig, Michael T. 1987. *Shamanism, Colonialism, and the Wild Man: A Study in Terror and Healing*. Chicago: University of Chicago Press.

Taussig, Michael T. 2011. *I Swear I Saw This: Drawings in Fieldwork Notebooks, Namely My Own*. Chicago: University of Chicago Press.

Terry, Jennifer. 2009. "Significant Injury: War, Medicine, and Empire in Claudia's Case." *Women's Studies Quarterly* 37 (1–2): 200–225.

Terry, Jennifer. 2017. *Attachments to War: Biomedical Logics and Violence in Twenty-First Century America.* Durham, NC: Duke University Press.

Thomas, Dylan. (1953) 2013. "My Hero Bares His Nerves." In *The Collected Poems of Dylan Thomas.* New York: New Directions.

Turner, Sarah. 2013. "Dilemmas and Detours: Fieldwork with Ethnic Minorities in Upland Southwest China, Vietnam, and Laos." In *Red Stamps and Gold Stars*, edited by Sarah Turner, 1–21. Vancouver: University of British Colombia Press.

Uk, Krisna. 2016. *Salvage: Cultural Resilience among the Jorai of Northeast Cambodia.* Ithaca, NY: Cornell University Press.

Warren, Kay B. 2000. "Conclusion: Death Squads and Wider Complicities: Dilemmas for the Anthropology of Violence." In *Death Squad: The Anthropology of State Terror*, edited by Jeffrey A. Sluka, 226–48. Philadelphia: University of Pennsylvania Press.

Williams, Rosalind. 2008. *Notes on the Underground: An Essay on Technology, Society, and the Imagination.* Cambridge, MA: MIT Press.

Wolfreys, Julian. 2013. "Preface: On Textual Haunting." In *The Spectralities Reader: Ghosts and Haunting in Contemporary Cultural Theory*, edited by Maria del Pilar Blanco and Esther Peeren, 69–74. New York: Bloomsbury Academic.

Wolters, O. W. 1999. *History, Culture, and Region in Southeast Asian Perspectives.* Ithaca, NY: Southeast Asian Program.

Zani, Leah. 2015. "Bomb Ecologies? Inhabiting Disability in Postconflict Laos." *Somatosphere*, June 29. http://somatosphere.net/2015/06/bomb-ecologies-inhabiting -disability-in-postconflict-laos.html.

Zani, Leah. n.d. "Poems and Fieldpoems." Unpublished manuscript.

Žižek, Slavoj. 2009. *The Parallax View.* Cambridge, MA: MIT Press.

Index

civil society: development in Laos and, 25–28; impact of state authoritarianism on, 140–44

clearance operations: affect relating to, 111–14; blast radius and, 101–6; bomb point in, 106–7; demolition process, 98–99; international humanitarian sector and, 19–21; at Lane Xang mine, 79–80; legal issues surrounding, 54, 59–61; in Old Sepon, 74–77; poverty alleviation and development and, 24–28; regional scrap trading and, 80–86; in Renovation period, 65–66; research methodology concerning, 28–34; in Sepon, 68. *See also* bomb ecologies

clothing, revival of older styles of, 28–29

cluster munitions: contamination in Laos from, 16–17; fruit metaphor for, 20–21; in Plain of Jars, 56–61; regional scrap trading in, 80–86; resale of gunpowder from, 17–18

Cold War, disappearances during, 135–36

Communist Brotherhood, fall of Soviet Union and, 22–23

conflict zones, sociality of, 6–8

contamination, remains and process of, 21

copper mining in Laos, 78–80

corporate clearance operators, battlefield clearance and, 20

cosmology in Laos, 5, 26–28, 35; disability and, 122–23; doubling in, 44–46; ecopolitics and, 48; ghosts in, 93; power and, 126–27; sound and, 116; urban development in Sepon and, 71–73

cucumber bomb (*laberd mak dtaeng*), 21

cultural studies: apprehensions about explosions in, 107–11; military waste in, 8–12; poetic parallelism and, 41–46; research methodology in, 30–34

Cyprus, postwar reconstruction as haunting in, 76–77

Daniel, E. V., 28–29

Darwish, Mahmoud, 62

data collection, research ethics and, 53–54

Daughtry, J. Martin, 117

deafness from demolitions, 115–17

deaths from bomb explosions, 107–11; resonant embodiment and, 123–27; spiritual power of, 121–23

Deleuze, Gilles, 82–83, 118

demolition process, 98–99; accidents compared with, 114–17; affect connected with, 111–14; plans for, 100–101; as postwar echo, 117–20

Derrida, Jacques, 66–68, 90–93

development: disappearance as haunting of, 137–40; in former bomb sites, 56–61; Lane Xang gold mine and, 78–80, 86–90; Laotian Renovation reforms and, 22–28; limitations in Laos of, 93–96; in socialist Asia, 46–48

disability: danger and, 14; victims' inhabitation of, 120–23

disappearance: as haunting development, 137–40; politics of, 135–37; of Sombath Somphone, 7–8, 35, 131–34

doubling, in Laos cosmology, 44–46

echo, postwar demolitions as, 117–20

El Salvador warfare model, 20

ethical attunement, apprehension and, 122–23

ethics in research, socially reinforced paranoia and, 53–54

ethnicity, Laotian concepts of, 88

ethnography: haunting of, 140–44; surveillance and, 47–48, 52–54

Evans, Grant, 22–23

explosions and explosives: apprehensions about, 107–11; apprehensions concerning, 102–6; blast radius of, 100–106; demolition of, 98–99; hauntings and role of, 83–86; nonhuman agency of, 13–21; regional stories about, 81–86; sociocultural effects of, 127–29; wartime vs. postwar explosions, 117–20. *See also* cluster munitions

faith-based development organizations, 25–28

farming, in cluster-bombed areas, 17–19

Faulkner, Sandra L., 61–62

fieldpoems, 61–64; ethnographic research and, 54–61

First Indochina War, 15

foreign investment in Laos, 65–68, 78–80

Foucault, Michel, 13

France, First Indochina War and, 15

Frank, Pat, 59, 98, 103

French, Lindsay, 121
French colonialism, in old Sepon, Laos, 69–73
fruit eaters, 5
funeral rituals: absence of, for bomb victims, 121–23; resonant embodiment in, 123–27; for Sombath, 139–40

galactic polity, Laotian economic development and, 23–28
Gammeltoft, Tine M., 121–22
Geertz, Clifford, 31–34, 58–59
Geneva Accords (1962), U.S. violation of, 15
Geneva International Centre for Humanitarian Demining, 20
geopolitics: development models and, 22–28; military waste and, 9–12; sedimentation of war and peace and, 7–8
ghosts: bomb victims as, 85–86; conceptual framework for, 91–93; demolitions as echoes of, 118–20; disability and, 121–23; at Lane Xang mine, 86–90; military waste in Laos and, 76–77; poems for, 124–27; resonant embodiment and, 123–27; Sepon ghost mine and, 80–86; war ghosts in Lao culture, 66–68
Glass Bees, The (Jünger), 65, 82–83
global markets, Laotian mines and, 90
gold, in Laos culture, 78–80
Good, Byron J., 67
Goodman, Steve, 102
Gordon, Avery, 92, 132
Guattari, Félix, 82–83, 118
Gustafsson, Mai Lan, 84–86, 93, 122–23

Hansen, Anne R., 26–28
Hansen, Mette H., 47–48
haunting: Derrida's concept of, 66–67, 90–91; disability and, 120–23; disappearance and, 137–40; military waste and theories of, 12–21, 66–68, 74–77, 90–93; postwar demolitions as echo and, 117–20; of postwar Vietnam, 84–85; revivals and, 22; in Sepon, 34–35, 65–68; war ghost in Lao culture and, 66–68
Henig, David, 10–11
High, Holly, 25–28, 47, 79, 89–90
Hirschkind, Charles, 122, 125
Ho Chi Minh Trail, 15, 66, 70, 79–80

human existence, power and instrumentalization of, 13
humanitarianism, clearance operations and, 20

imperialism: disability and, 121–23; disappearances and, 135–36; material remains of, 21
inert bombs, 119–20
injury, state of, 119–20
international development organizations, 25–28; phaseout of, 35
international humanitarian sector, "Laos model" of warfare and, 19–20
intervention, Secret War and logic of, 19–21
Iraq, El Salvador warfare model in, 20

Jakobson, Roman, 41, 43–44
jaleun (Laotian spiritual and material development), 24–28; urban renovation and, 72–73
Japan, occupation of Laos by, 15
Johnson, Andrew A., 83, 95
Jünger, Ernst, 65, 82–83

Khammouane Province, 28
Kim, Elena, 11
knowledge production, ethics of research and, 53–54
Korean DMZ, 11
Koret, Peter, 39, 41, 45
Kwon, Heonik, 84, 93, 122–23

Ladwig, Patrice, 77
land mines: in Sepon, 70–72; stockpiling in Laos of, 24
Lane Xang Hom Khao (Land of a Million Elephants and the White Parasol), 79–80
Lane Xang Metals Limited mine (Lane Xang gold mine), 66–68, 78–80, 84–86; development and role of, 86–90
Lao Communist Party, 22–23
Lao Front for Socialist Construction, 25
Laos: Buddhist monks' role in postwar revival of, 126–27; civil war in, 15; economic development in, 24–28; Japanese occupation in World War II, 15; market-oriented development in, 67–68; Renovation reform period in, 7–8, 22–23; sociality of battlefields in, 6–8; unexploded ordnance in, 15–16; U.S. covert bombing in, 15

Phou Tai ethnic group, 87–88, 94
pineapple bomb (*laberd mak nad*), 21, 81–86
Plain of Jars (Xieng Khouang Province),
    55–61
poetic parallelism, resonant embodiment and,
    123–27
poetry: ethnography and, 33–34; fieldpoems,
    54–61; Lao parallelism in, 38–39, 41–46;
    "pattern of three" in, 45–46; war poetry,
    61–64
police harassment: disappearance of Sombath
    Somphone and, 135–36; of ethnographic
    research, 47–48, 52–54; fieldwork in South-
    east Asia and, 49–52, 132–34; impact on
    fieldwork of, 142–44; paranoia in Laos over,
    40–41; routinization of, 145–47
Ponesse, Julie, 54
post-Soviet scholarship, fieldwork in socialist
    Asia and, 46
power: of death, 13; military waste as exten-
    sion of, 129; sound of explosion as, 35;
    Southeast Asian religious concepts of,
    126–27
precarity, disability and, 120–23
privatization, development models and, 23–28
Puar, Jasbir K., 14, 120–21

Reid, Anthony J., 26
religion: development and, 25–28; explosions
    and, 121–23; poetic parallelism and, 42–46;
    Southeast Asian concepts of power and,
    126–27
remains: conceptual framework for, 12–21; de-
    fined, 12; development and cycle of, 94–96;
    hauntology of, 91–93; Lane Xang gold mine
    and, 78–80; sedimentation of war and peace
    and, 7–8; Sepon postwar reconstruction
    and, 74–77
Renovation reform period (Laos), 7–8, 22–23,
    65; ambivalence in Sepon toward, 73; Lane
    Xang gold mine and, 68; rural marginal
    areas and, 66
research methodology: anthropology of terror
    and, 144–47; clearance operations and,
    28–34; fieldwork in socialist Asia, 46–48;
    impact of paranoia on, 140–44
resonant embodiment, bomb explosions and,
    123–27

revivals: authoritarianism in Laos and,
    40–41; development and cycle of, 94–96;
    Lane Xang gold mine and, 78–80; parallel
    framework for, 22–28; remains and, 12–21;
    sedimentation of war and peace and, 7–8;
    Sepon postwar reconstruction and, 74–77
Rilke, Rainer Maria, 63
risk: disability and, 120–23; mine risk educa-
    tion training, 124–27; in mining operations,
    88–90; necropolitics and concepts of, 14; in
    research fieldwork, 52–54
Robben, Antonius C. G. M., 139
rogue infrastructure, military waste and, 11
ruins and ruination, scholarship on, 21
Russell, Elaine, 67
Russia, military waste in Laos from, 15

Salavan Province, 28, 100
Savannakhet Province, 28–30, 66–68, 95–96
scrap trading, in rural Laos, 80–86
Second Indochina War. *See* Vietnam-American
    War
secrecy, ethnographic research and need for,
    52–54
Secret War (Laos): abductions during, 133–34;
    CIA operation of, 6–8, 15–16; disappear-
    ances and, 136; as social and cultural
    intervention, 19–21
Sedgwick, Eve Kosofsky, 51
sensory effects of explosions, 114–17
Sepon, Laos: foreign organizations in, 68;
    ghost mine in, 80–86; haunting of, 34,
    66–68, 90–93; parallel urban centers in,
    69–73; postwar development in, 23–24,
    74–80, 95–96
Shread, Carolyn, 82–83
Simpson, Audra, 61
Singh, Sarinda, 73
situated ethics, 53–54
slow violence, processes of, 6
smoothing process, postwar revival and,
    126–27
socialist Asia, ethnographic fieldwork in,
    46–48
sociality of war, 6–8
socioeconomic liberalization: Renovation
    reforms in Laos and, 7–8; in socialist Asia,
    46–48

Sombath Somphone: abduction of, 7–8, 35, 131–34, 137; haunting presence of, 140–44; life and work of, 134–35; video recording of disappearance of, 134–35

sound: affect connected with, 111–14; apprehensions and, 107–11; effects of explosions and, 100–106; resonant embodiment and, 123–27; sociocultural effects of, 127–29

South America, disappearances in, 132, 135–37, 139

Southeast Asia: military waste and war ghosts in, 67–68; religious concepts of power in, 126–27; war-related disability in, 121

sovereignty, Laotian religious concepts of, 26–28

Soviet Union: Afghanistan conflict and, 20; Laos and fall of, 22–23

"spectre of comparisons," 22

specular violence, postwar demolitions as, 119–20

spirit possession events, at Lane Xang mine, 86–90

spiritual power: development and, 24–28; injury and disability from explosions and, 121–23; resonant embodiment and, 123–27

state authority: clearance operations and role of, 24; development in Laos and, 25–28; disappearances and, 136; impact on research of, 140–44; post-Communist development and, 46–48; research and avoidance of, 52–54; resurrection of past and, 89–90

Sterne, Jonathan, 112

stigmatization of bomb victims, 120

Stoler, Ann Laura, 21

Study Information Letter, 49–50

subterranean consciousness, at Lane Xang mine, 89–90

surveillance: disappearance and, 139–40; of ethnographic research, 47–48, 52–54; fieldwork in Southeast Asia and, 49–52; impact on fieldwork of, 142–44; paranoia in Laos over, 40–41

sweaty concepts, 32

Taussig, Michael T., 136

technological progress, military waste as barrier to, 86–90

technologies of war, Secret War and development of, 19–21

terror: anthropology of, 144–47; disappearances and culture of, 136; impact on fieldwork of, 142; Lao culture of, 40–41; normalization of, 28–29

Thailand: literature in, 41; market-oriented development in, 67–68; occupation of Laos by, 15

That Luang stupa, images of, 26–27

Theravada Buddhism: disability and cosmology of, 121–23; Laotian economic development and, 23–28; resonant embodiment in poetry of, 123–27

thick description, 30–34

thin description, 31–34

trauma of bomb explosions, 107–11

Turner, Sarah, 46–47

unexploded ordnance (UXO): defined, 12; nonhuman agency of, 13

UN General Assembly, 135–36

unsounded ethnography, 102–6

urban life, Laos cosmology and, 71–73

UXO Survivor Information Centre, 114–17, 119

victim assistance, disability studies and, 14, 120–23

Vientiane, Laos, Western development in, 46–48

Vietnam, spectre of disability in, 121–23

Vietnam-American War, 15; anthropologists as spies during, 49–52; destruction of Plain of Jars during, 55; explosions during, 118; Lane Xang gold mine during, 79–80; language of accidents and, 83; victims of disability after, 121

violence: affect connected with, 111–14; in anthropological research, 59–61; demolitions as echo of, 117–20; language of accidents and, 83–86

vitalism, 12

war: affect connected with, 111–14; in anthropological research, 59–61; Deleuze and Guattari on, 82–83; demolitions as echo of, 117–20; explosions during, 117–20; "Laos

model" of warfare and, 19–20, 136; remains in Sepon of, 74–77; sociality of, 6–8
war ghost in Lao culture, 66–68
Wat Sepon Gao (Old Sepon Temple), 69–70, 72–77, 94
Wat Sokpaluang, 3–4

Williams, Rosalind, 86, 89, 96
Wolfreys, Julian, 92–93
World Bank, Laotian economic development and, 23

Xieng Khouang Province, 28, 55–61